THE JESUS OBSESSION

ELTON F. CHESSER

THE JESUS OBSESSION

ELTON F. CHESSER

Scriptures unless otherwise marked are taken from the KING JAMES VERSION (KJV): KING JAMES VERSION, public domain.

ISBN 978-1-961482-28-9

"That I may know him, and the power of his resurrection, and the fellowship of his sufferings, being made conformable unto his death; if by any means I might attain unto the resurrection of the dead."

Apostle Paul

Dedicated to the memory of my dear friend and pastor, Bishop Clint Barnes, who was completely obsessed with knowing Jesus.

Preface

How would a person's life be so greatly affected if he (or she) would determine to become obsessed with knowing Jesus. To dedicate every waking moment to giving every breath to Him. To love as He loved, to forgive as He forgave, and to share the gospel of the Kingdom with everyone. Not only living it in front of them but sharing their testimony with them as well.

If we follow Jesus only when it is convenient for us, are we really serving Him? Do we even love Him if our love is conditional? To know Him in the depths of a relationship in which I believe He desires us, we must be immersed in Him... obsessed with Him.

In this book, I attempt to show how several Biblical characters lived once they determined to obsessively know and serve Jesus. I also share what I consider to be practical applications in making this obsession possible. My goal is to inspire the reader to join those of us who are obsessed with Jesus.

Sincerely,
Elton F. Chesser

Foreword

We were thrilled when Elton asked us to read his latest book. The subject piqued our interest because "obsession" is often overused (or misused) in our culture.

I (Carla) have known Elton my entire life. We are first cousins from a large, close-knit family (there are 34 first cousins). There are so many funny stories I could tell about Elton, but what stands out above all is his love for people, especially his love for sharing the Word of God with them. If he is not teaching a Home Bible Study, he is looking for someone to teach. He personifies Mark 12:30-31; he loves the Lord, and he loves people.

I (Phil) am always interested in personal stories centered on Biblical themes. I enjoyed how Elton gave solid Biblical teaching and applied it to modern spiritual situations. He discusses 21st-century problems and applies 1st-century Bible instruction. I applaud his remaining true to Bible teachings. He doesn't shy away from the hard facts. We started our ministries around the same time in the late 1970s, and although our paths took different directions, the Lord bound us together with a love for the Gospel and people.

This book combines Biblical history, biographies, and teachings that can be applied at any stage of the reader's spiritual journey. It is filled with sound, Biblical doctrine to guide our Christian disciplines. Not just a guide, but a challenge to us as followers of Jesus to take on the obsession that drove the apostles and early believers, no matter the cost. We believe you will finish this book with a renewed determination to follow Christ and make Him your obsession.

Elton writes in a way that makes the reader feel as if he is sitting "across the table," sharing food, fellowship, and the Word. No condescending tones or difficult words and concepts, just a warm, friendly tone that makes the Biblical truths less difficult to swallow.

And, if you know the author personally, you know a few jokes and stories that will sweeten the visit.

We encourage you to read The Jesus Obsession slowly, prayerfully, and with a heart open to hear the voice of the One who died for us. We savored each chapter over coffee as a morning devotion, sparking many thought-provoking discussions and giving us the resolve to let Jesus be our greatest obsession. We pray it will impact your life and that you will become “obsessed” with Jesus. He is the only One worthy.

Phil and Carla DePriest

Bishop, Centerpointe Apostolic Church

Murfreesboro, Tennessee

Contents

Section One
Biblical Examples

Chapter One

Peter, the Apostle

(Also known as Simon, Simon Bar-Jona, Cephas)

The story of Simon Peter is the story of a man with strong personality and drive but needing direction. The first introduction of Peter to Jesus is told in the first Chapter of the Gospel of John.

Andrew, Peter's brother, being a disciple of John the Baptist was with John when Jesus happened to walk by one day. John declared Jesus to be "the Lamb of God, which taketh away the sin of the World." Intrigued, two of John's disciples left him and began to follow Jesus as he walked. One of the two, according to John, was Andrew.

After the encounter with Jesus, Andrew found his brother Peter and told him, "We have found the Messiah" and brought Peter to meet Jesus. What an interesting introduction it was. Andrew bringing Peter and introducing him to Jesus, and the first words out of the mouth of Jesus were, "Thou art Simon the son of Jona: thou shalt be called Cephas." Cephas, being interpreted, meant "a stone."

To understand the desire and commitment Peter had toward Jesus, we must understand the turning point. The place in Peter's heart when everything changed.

Still early in the ministry of Jesus, He took his disciples and they stood by the lake of Gennesaret (Sea of Galilee) where the people had pressed to hear the word of God. Jesus, climbing aboard Peter's boat, asked him to cast out a little way from the shore, and there Jesus taught the people.

After Jesus was finished teaching, he directed Peter to launch out into the deep waters and cast his net. Peter explained that he had fished all night and had caught nothing but, because it was a request of Jesus, Peter did as he was asked.

Suddenly, the net was overwhelmed by a great multitude of fish. So much so, that the net began to break. Peter requested help from the other ship belonging to James and John, who were partnered with him. As the ships were taking in this amazing catch of fish, both ships were so full they began to sink. It was at that moment something clicked inside Peter, and he would never be the same. Being "astonished" at what he had just experienced, he fell at the feet of Jesus and said, "Depart from me; for I am a sinful man, O Lord" (Luke 1:8).

If we truly have a desire to fully know Jesus as he would have us know him, this is step one. It is an incredibly humbling experience but one that must occur. We must come to the realization that, left on our own, we are sinful creatures. This is the awakening that drives the alcoholic and drug addict to seek deliverance. It drives near-broken marriages to godly counsel and prayer. It drives someone who wishes they had the strength to follow Jesus to go all in.

And go all in, Peter did!

Oh, I know Simon Peter, the "Rock," failed after Gethsemane while warming himself by the fire. But we'll get to that in a bit. This moment changed Peter.

I'm not a psychiatrist, nor psychologist, but I have dealt with various types of people my entire life. I see something in the personality of Peter that I have seen in a few people I have met in my lifetime and in my ministry.

To me, Peter has always seemed to have a Type A personality. If you research "Type A" personality, you will uncover something like the following, Type A personality is a behavioral pattern characterized by:

- Competitiveness
- Ambition
- Time Urgency
- High-Strung
- High Achieving Nature

Does that sound like Apostle Peter, or what? It may sound like someone in your life, or perhaps even you. Peter was the one who, in John chapter twenty-one, jumped out of the boat and swam to shore rather than simply waiting for the boat to hit land. On the Day of Pentecost when the apostles were asked, "What shall we do?" Peter did not hesitate, in the event someone else wanted to answer the question. Peter spoke right up and gave us one of the most quoted scriptures in the Bible: Acts 2:38.

Early in the ministry of Jesus, Matthew tells of a day when, as Jesus walked by the Sea of Galilee, He came upon Peter (and his brother Andrew) casting a net into the water. Jesus said to them, "Follow me, and I will make you fishers of men." They immediately left their nets and followed Jesus. This is what one does when one wants to know Christ. If we become obsessed with knowing Him, it would cause us to rearrange our priorities. We would situate our lives so that He was at the top of the list and everything else would come after. Yes, family time is important. Raising children, working, doing all the chores of life that must be done are crucial. Even vacations and time to rest and relax are important. But none of these other facets of life can compare to knowing Jesus. Truly knowing Him.

Matthew the publican, one of the twelve apostles chosen by Jesus, wrote in his gospel about a time when Jesus brought his twelve in for a talk. Jesus was going to send them out to minister in the Jewish cities in the area, so He gave them commands. He sent them to the lost sheep of Israel. He instructed them, "as ye go, preach, saying, the kingdom of heaven is at hand. Heal the sick, cleanse the leper, raise the dead, cast out devils: freely ye have received, freely give" (Matthew 10:7-8). There were many other teachings and commandments Jesus gave them before He sent them out, but let's look at these.

Remember, we're talking about a group of ordinary men who, for the most part, had very ordinary jobs. Simon Peter, the subject of this chapter, was a fisherman. In his day, Peter had to know he would never become wealthy being a common fisherman, and apparently Peter did not have the strongest of education since the rulers, elders and scribes in Acts chapter four noted he (and John) seemed unlearned and ignorant.

Now please don't misunderstand me. I'm not criticizing Peter. I want us to understand that when Jesus chose His twelve, He did not pick the elite. He did not pick the wealthy nor the affluent. He chose twelve men, no matter how seemingly common or ordinary, who would submerge themselves in Him. That is what Jesus still looks for.

With that being said, let's take another look at what Jesus commanded Peter and the rest of the apostles. Heal the sick, cleanse the lepers, raise the dead, and cast out devils. Seriously? He sent them out on a solo mission if you will, without HIM. Jesus sent them out, away from Him, commanding them to do these miracles. Raise the dead? I've seen many healings and miracles in my life. I've seen devils cast out. I've even heard of a few people being raised from the dead, although I've not seen it with my own eyes. Jesus sent them out to perform these things as though He was sending them to the grocery store.

Why are we, at times, surprised when Jesus heals a person right in front of us? Why do we wrestle with demonic spirits when they need to be cast out? Why aren't all the gifts of the Spirit used regularly in our churches? I contend that the power of the Holy Ghost, deliverance, healing, and the gifts of the Spirit should be commonplace in our church services and in our lives. Jesus said before He ascended, these signs shall follow them that believe. It takes knowing Him: truly, deeply, knowing Him. Some things come only through prayer and fasting.

Can you imagine the lift in Peter's spirit as he laid hands on sick people and they were healed? Commanding devils to flee, and they scattered. Perhaps Peter even raised a dead person or two since that's what Jesus instructed them to do. Peter is flying high now. He has committed his will to the will of God, and in return Jesus has given him power in heaven.

The fame of Jesus scattered abroad, even to the point that Herod believed John the Baptist had resurrected. Jesus continued to heal the sick and teach the people. After feeding the five thousand men, beside women and children (Matthew 14), Jesus went up to the mountain to pray while the apostles got into a ship. When the evening had come, and it was well toward sunrise, a storm came and began to blow the ship and the sea. The apostles looked, and they saw Jesus walking on the water to join them. Peter, that Type A personality guy, shouted, "Lord, if it be Thou, bid me to come unto thee on the water." The Lord invited him to come, and Peter stepped off the boat and onto the sea.

You are probably familiar with the story. Peter steps out onto the waves, and begins to walk on the water, but when the wind is boisterous, it scares Peter and he becomes afraid and begins to sink. He yells for the Lord to save him, and the Lord lifts him up out of the water and then rebukes him, saying, "O thou of little faith, wherefore didst thou doubt?" One translation says, "Why did you doubt?"

You would think a man who, not long ago took the command of Jesus and went out and healed many sick folks, cast out devils, and raised a corpse or two would never doubt again. Doesn't that sound just like the human condition?

I know Jesus rebuked Peter, and rightly so, and I have heard preachers over the years give Peter their own righteous indignation, but I have always felt differently about the entire situation. Simon Peter is the only one of the twelve who had enough nerve and faith to even give it a try. Where were Andrew, James, and John? Where was Matthew, the tax collector in the group? How about the man who held the money for the group? I find it very difficult to give Peter a hard time about losing faith when there were eleven other men on that boat who sat silently in the back. I heard a Christian comedian say years ago, "I want to be doing something for the Lord when He comes, even if it's just making mistakes."

Let me share my take on this event. There was something deep inside Peter that, when he saw Jesus walking on the water, he desired to do it too. Maybe it was the drive of that Type A personality, but maybe it was that he was so entrenched on being like Jesus that he literally wanted to do what Christ did. I would like to think that if I had been present, I would have cheered Peter on. Come on Peter, you can do it!!! At least you tried.

Maybe you don't have the outgoing, strong personality that Peter had. I know some are more comfortable to be quiet in the back and happy to let others lead. But I am convinced that when we truly desire to know Him, it will drive us to be everything He calls us to be. Some will be evangelists, some will be singers, some will quietly teach children in Sunday school class, while changing tomorrow for them. It all fits neatly together.

A multitude sought Jesus after He had fed the thousands, and He began to teach them. John, in his gospel in chapter six, tells all the things Jesus said that day. He began to get deep, and many didn't understand what He was saying. Finally, many began to grumble that what Jesus was teaching was hard. Many followers stopped following Jesus that day.

The exodus of so many people was quite obvious. Seeing much of the crowd turn and walk away, Jesus turned to the twelve and asked, "Will you also go away?" Peter once again was the one who spoke up. But by doing so, we know by his declaration that Peter understood. "Lord, to whom shall we go? Thou hast the words of eternal life. And we believe and are sure that thou art the Christ, the Son of the Living God."

The Word of God doesn't tell us, but I can't help but believe that Jesus felt some satisfaction that His words were getting through to the twelve. Jesus knew, before He would ascend into heaven, those men must know who He is and have it in their hearts. Peter knew.

> And supper being ended, the devil having now put into the heart of Judas Iscariot, Simon's son, to betray him. Jesus knowing that the Father had given all things into his hands, and that he was come from God, and went to God; he riseth from supper and laid aside his garments; and took a towel and girded himself. After he poureth water into a bason, and began to wash the disciples' feet, and to wipe them with the towel wherewith he was girded. Then cometh he to Simon Peter: and Peter saith unto him, Lord, dost thou wash my feet? Jesus answered and said unto him, What I do thou knowest not now; but thou shalt know hereafter. Peter saith unto him; Thou shalt never wash my feet. Jesus answered him, If I wash thee not, thou hast no part with me. Simon Peter saith unto him, Lord, not my feet only, but also my hands and my head.
>
> John 13:2-19. KJV

This portion of the Scripture depicting Jesus washing the feet of the disciples has always made me smile inside. Jesus was making a point to the twelve that just as servants humble themselves and wash the feet of those coming into homes, we, as the children of God, must humble ourselves and serve each other. Obviously, Peter had not yet figured this part out.

Can you imagine how appalled Peter must have felt while watching some of the other apostles allow Jesus to wash their feet? Finally, Jesus gets to Peter. Lord, you will never wash my feet. It's not going to happen. I can understand Peter's thoughts. Here's the Savior of the World. I need Him. I'm lost without Him. And now He thinks I'm going to allow Him to be a servant to me and wash my feet? Nope. But Peter is challenged in a way he did not see coming. Peter, you don't understand now, but you will soon. If you don't allow me to wash you, then you have no part with me. Are you kidding, Lord? I've cast out devils in your Name. I've laid hands on the sick like you, and they were healed. In you is eternal life. I'm not missing out on this. So, Peter did as Peter was prone to do. Maybe overreact a little? "Then Lord, not only my feet, but my hands and my head also." In other words, if this is what it takes to be a part of you, then let's just go all in. Peter wanted to show the Lord he was all in, and he must have all of Him. Serving the Lord is not always comfortable, but it is necessary.

After the Passover and the washing of feet, Jesus led the apostles, now eleven, since Judas left to make his way to the Chief Priests, over the brook Cedron, to the garden. After some much agonizing prayer, a throng of soldiers, chief priests, and Pharisees approached to find Jesus and arrest Him. It's John, in his gospel in chapter eighteen, who tells us it is none other than Simon Peter who, in defense of his Lord, draws his sword and severs the right ear of Malchus, the servant of the high priest. Jesus heals the servant, and tells Peter to put away his sword, because He must drink of the cup which the Father gave Him. It wasn't really a rebuke, but an explanation to Peter, I've got to do what I've come here to do.

But can you blame Peter? Really! Peter has given three and one-half years to get where he is in Christ. He met the Messiah face to face and made up his mind to follow Him at any cost. I question people who live with no passion for anything. Even if we are not an outgoing, outspoken person, can't we get passionate about what Jesus has done for us? I don't blame you, Peter. I'd like to think I would have done the same thing.

They led Jesus to Caiaphas, and all the disciples forsook Jesus, but Peter followed afar off all the way to the priest's palace, sitting amid some of the servants to observe. While Jesus was being questioned and lied about, Peter watched from afar, at one point warming himself by the fire. First, it was what Matthew in chapter twenty-six describes as a damsel who recognized Peter. Then a maid came by and recognized him. Lastly, some who had been standing by recognized him and he again began to curse and deny it.

The gospel writer, Luke, describes the scene. "And the Lord turned and looked upon Peter. And Peter remembered the word of the Lord, how he had said unto him, Before the cock crow, thou shalt deny me thrice. And Peter went out and wept bitterly" (Luke 22:61-62).

Can you imagine the deep, crushing blow Peter must have felt in his spirit. Especially given the fact that after failing, Jesus turned and looked right at him. I cringe every time I think about it. Peter, no doubt, was embarrassed and horribly disappointed and angry with himself. To work forty-two months to gain the power of Christ. To achieve the ability to heal the sick and cast out devils just as Jesus, and to throw it all away in one moment of fear. But here's some good news. Jesus forgives and restores.

Who among us has never failed? Perhaps it wasn't as open and obvious as Peter's failure, but still a failure. How fitting that Peter would later write:

> But ye are a chosen generation, a royal priesthood, an holy nation, a peculiar people; that ye should

> shew forth the praises of him who hath called you out of darkness into his marvelous light; which in time past were not a people, but are now the people of God: which had not obtained mercy, but now have obtained mercy.
>
> I Peter 2:9-10

After the resurrection, Jesus showed Himself to the disciples forty days before ascending into heaven. According to John's account, the third time Jesus showed Himself to the apostles, they were eating together when Jesus asked Peter, "Simon, son of Jonas, lovest thou me more than these?" Peter said, "Yea, Lord, thou knowest that I love thee." After Jesus asked the same question, a second and third time, Peter was grieved and replied, "Lord, thou knowest all things; thou knowest that I love thee." Jesus replied, "Feed my sheep." Jesus was soon going to ascend into heaven, and He was turning the reins of the church, that was soon to be born, into the hands of the apostles, especially Peter. The past forty-two months had at times been challenging, but these men were ready.

> Then opened he their understanding that they might understand the scriptures, and said unto them, Thus it is written, and thus it behooved Christ to suffer, and to rise from the dead the third day; and that repentance and remission of sins should be preached in his name among all nations, beginning at Jerusalem. And ye are witnesses of these things. And behold, I send the promise of my Father upon you; but tarry ye in the city of Jerusalem, until ye be endued with power from on high.
>
> Luke 24:45-49

Peter, with the other apostles and believers, returned to Jerusalem where they were continually in the upper room together seeking the promise of the Father. Jesus had told them before ascending into heaven that they would receive power after that the Holy Ghost had come upon them. After continuing prayer and fellowship for about seven days, the power of the Holy Ghost fell upon Peter and the others. Luke tells us there were about one hundred twenty in the upper room who were filled that day.

> And when the day of Pentecost was fully come, they were all with one accord in one place. And suddenly there came a sound from heaven as of a rushing mighty wind, and it filled all the house where they were sitting. And there appeared unto them cloven tongues like as of fire, and it sat upon each of them. And they were all filled with the Holy Ghost, and began to speak with other tongues, as the Spirit gave them utterance.
>
> Acts 2:1-4

Simon Peter, who had seen the highs of laying hands on the sick and seeing them recover when Jesus had sent them out, and seen the lows of failing and weeping bitterly, had now received the ultimate power and gift of God. This is what Peter had been striving for since Andrew had first introduced him to Jesus. What a winding road it had been. Peter had stuck close to Jesus and now it's going to pay off greater than ever.

When we decide to follow Jesus, it will certainly change our direction. But knowing Jesus fully is a process that takes time. In my teen years, a friend of mine received the gift of the Holy Ghost in his very first apostolic church service. But to be taught, comprehend the ways of God, and apply it to all facets of his life took time. Those forty-two months Peter spent with Jesus was a process he needed to go through to reach this point.

Peter would be tested immediately!

The Word of God tells us that as those one hundred twenty people received the Holy Ghost, they were making quite a commotion. It gained the attention of the thousands of men who had converged upon Jerusalen for the Feast of Pentecost. Many mocked them believing they were drunk. Others questioned all the noise and carrying on. Peter, having just received the Comforter as Jesus had promised, was moved with boldness and began to preach to the throng, explaining what was happening, even charging them that it was by their wicked hands that Jesus had been crucified and slain.

As a side note, let me say that I believe preachers today need to be bolder and truly tell the people what they need to hear. In a world full of churches and ministries that just tell people they're fine, we need men who will preach the Word without fear.

It's interesting to note that the first four times Peter preached or explained his stance concerning Jesus in the Book of Acts, he charged his listeners by telling them, they were the ones who crucified the Lord of glory. You'll notice it brought either an attack upon Peter or great repentance from those hearing his words.

By the end of the Day of Pentecost, three thousand new converts were baptized in Jesus' name. Peter moved into the role of one of the pastors of this new, great work and continued to preach and teach, baptizing new converts, and the church grew daily.

There came a day when Peter and his dear friend, John, were about to enter the temple for the hour of prayer. Luke writes about this event in the third chapter of Acts. It's interesting to note that they were not leaving after having a prayer hour, but rather they were entering. They had not yet had this great prayer meeting together. A man was laying at the gate, which was called, Beautiful, begging alms. Notice the actions of Peter, a man who had been striving to know Jesus completely and fully. Peter approaches the lame man and says, "Look on us." When you are fully engulfed with the will of God and knowing Him, you'll never worry about who gets the credit. Peter included John as he addressed the lame man, look on us. One man does not win an entire city. One man does not bring revival to a church. But one man, when he does not care who gets the credit, can be a catalyst for great things to happen.

After explaining to the lame man that he has no money to give him, he offered to give him of what he did have. Peter reached down and took the man's right hand and lifted him up. Now it may sound humorous, but I have always said, if you're going to grab a lame man by the hand and lift him up, you better be incredibly certain God is going to heal him, or you'll throw that man right on his face. "In the name of Jesus Christ of Nazareth rise up and walk" Peter commanded, and the lame man rose up and began to leap and walk and praise God.

That frustrated, brokenhearted apostle who ran from the face of Jesus and wept bitterly less than two months ago, had just been used in several of the gifts of the Spirit. Peter had the gift of faith, and through that faith, he and John saw an amazing miracle of healing. Peter achieved his goal. He could finally say, I truly, deeply know Him.

Peter went on to build the church in Jerusalem into thousands. Through a vison in Acts chapter ten, Peter brought the gospel to the Gentile world, seeing Cornelius and his entire household receive the Holy Ghost and speak in tongues as the apostles had on the day of Pentecost, commanding them all to be baptized in Jesus' name.

If you had told Peter on the night Jesus was crucified that he, Peter, would be instrumental in building a great church in Jerusalem, bringing the gospel to the Gentiles, writing books, and taking the gospel to Israel, he would not have believed you. Looking over Peter's life and ministry, what made the greatest difference was the day he received the power of the Holy Ghost, speaking in tongues as the Spirit gave him power.

The story of Peter is one of strength through brokenness. Grace covering failure, and transformation into a powerful witness. It's a story of perseverance and never giving up. We will have our ups and downs and failures, but every day is a new day with a new challenge.

If you want to know Jesus, truly know Him, the greatest difference is when you allow Him to fill you with the gift of the Holy Ghost. It will be a life changer for you, just as it was for Peter.

> Beloved, think it not strange concerning the fiery trial which is to try you, as though some strange thing happened unto you: but rejoice, inasmuch as ye are partakers of Christ's sufferings; that, when his glory shall be revealed, ye may be glad also with exceeding joy.
>
> I Peter 4:12-13

Chapter Two

Nathanael, the Apostle

(Also known as Bartholomew, Aramaic for Son of Tolmai)

Little is revealed to us concerning Nathanael in the Gospels, and as a matter of fact, he's usually called Bartholomew. But I wanted to include him due to the way he came to Jesus. His story is told in the first chapter of the Gospel of John. The day after Andrew met Jesus and brought his brother Peter to meet him, Jesus found Philip, who would become an apostle, and instructed him, "follow me."

Philip, in his excitement to have found the Messiah sought out his dear friend Nathanael, and told him, "We have found him, of whom Moses in the law, and the prophets, did write, Jesus of Nazareth, the son of Joseph." Nathanael was not impressed.

"Can there any good thing come out of Nazareth?" Ouch! Not sure what was happening in Nazareth that had Nathanael so turned off, but regardless, he wasn't buying it. "Come and see," was Philip's response.

We live in a time when many souls are turned off by the religious people who claim to know Him but really don't. Preachers who claim to represent Christ, who haven't spoken to Him in years. No wonder we have a large contingency of people who were once interested in knowing Jesus but are interested no longer. People have been scammed, lied to, or misled, and it leaves a long-lasting hurt in their spirit. I can't say I blame them. If we are going to win people to Christ, we need to really know Christ, know His Word, and love those who need Him.

As Philip, in his excitement, led Nathanael to Jesus, Jesus already had his eye on Nathanael. "Behold an Israelite indeed, in whom is no guile!" What an odd thing to say to an individual the first time you meet them. How do you know me? Jesus explained to Nathanael, that, "Before that Philip called thee, when thou wast under the fig tree, I saw thee."

I'm not exactly sure what snapped inside the heart and mind of Nathanael when Jesus said those words, but Nathanael's attitude suddenly changed. "Rabbi, thou art the Son of God; thou art the King of Israel." Jesus seemed to be a little surprised by Nathanael's exclamation, but can anyone really ever catch Jesus off guard? Jesus responded, "Because I said unto thee, I saw thee under the fig tree, believest thou? Thou shalt see greater things than these."

Now here's the reason I wanted to include Nathanael. It was what Jesus said next, and the implication that came along with it. In John 1:51, the last verse of that chapter, Jesus says to Nathanael, "Verily, verily, I say unto you, Hereafter ye shall see heaven open, and the angels of God ascending and descending upon the Son of man."

In other words, Nathanael, if you think the fact that I knew you was an amazing thing, just wait until you see what's next. Nathanael had no idea how his life was about to change. In one day, he went from being a common ordinary man, good friends with Philip, to being called by the Messiah.

In the next forty two months, Nathanael saw the deaf healed, the lame walk, a man's withered hand healed, the blind healed, demons cast out, lepers cleansed, the woman with an issue of blood healed, Peter's mother in-law healed of fever, Lazarus raised from the dead, Jesus walking on water, thousands of people fed with just a few loaves of bread and a few fish, and Jesus calm a storm. Not to mention the miracles that Nathanael himself performed when Jesus sent them out into the cities to heal the sick and perform miracles.

Nathanael gave himself to Jesus for forty-two months and it was life-changing. He was there in the upper room on the day of Pentecost when the Holy Ghost fell, and everyone began to speak in other tongues. He was there backing Peter up as Peter preached the first apostolic Holy Ghost filled message to the thousands gathered for Pentecost. He was there as the church in Jerusalem grew and all the apostles who had stayed in the city took part in the daily ministries.

When Nathanael realized who Jesus was, he determined to know Him and know Him he did!

Can I challenge you today? If you don't know Jesus the way you would like, or maybe all these things are new to you, give yourself to Him for forty-two months and see if He won't change your life. If you will commit to give yourself to Jesus for the next forty-two months with the purpose of knowing Him deeper than ever before, I am certain that you will be a different person at the end of that three and one-half years.

> "He that believeth on me, as the scripture hath said,
> out of his belly shall flow rivers of living water."
>
> Jesus
>
> John 7:38

Chapter Three

Stephen

(A man full of faith and of the Holy Ghost)

The story of Stephen in the New Testament is short, and what we may consider tragic in our fleshly eyes, but there's much to learn about the way Stephen knew Jesus.

After the Holy Ghost was poured out on the day of Pentecost, the church continued to grow by great numbers. So much so, that the apostles couldn't keep up with ministering to all the people. There arose a conflict between the Grecians and the Hebrews, because their widows were being neglected in the daily ministration. The Grecians were Jews who spoke Greek, many times living outside Judea, and they had a Greek influence. So, there was somewhat of a culture clash, even though they were also the descendants of the tribes of Israel.

After the apostles conferred, they presented a plan. They told the many disciples to choose seven men who were of honest report, full of the Holy Ghost, and wisdom, and the apostles would appoint the seven over the daily ministration. In doing so, the apostles could continue in teaching and preaching the Word of God.

One of the men chosen was Stephen who Luke, the author of the book of Acts, described as a man full of faith and of the Holy Ghost. Luke does not describe Stephen as a preacher, but we can see by his accomplishments that he did certainly teach and debate in an effort to win souls to Christ. He was not one of the twelve apostles, but he was simply a faithful servant, who Luke tells us in Acts 6:8 did "great wonders and miracles among the people."

May I become sidetracked for a moment and remind us that when we receive our reward from Jesus, he is not going to say, "Well done my good and faithful preacher, or teacher, or singer, or usher." He's going to say, "Well done thou good and faithful servant." It doesn't matter what your position in the Kingdom of God is. The Lord will take prayerful, faithful servants and do great things through them.

There came a day when some of the people of the synagogue began to dispute with Stephen but Stephen, being full of wisdom and of the Holy Ghost, spoke truthfully and boldly concerning Jesus. When these men of the synagogue saw that they could not win an argument or debate against Stephen, they encouraged some to lie and say that they had heard Stephen speak blasphemous words against Moses and against God, and they stirred up the people, the elders and the scribes. Isn't this the case even today? When people disagree with us, they at times begin to lie or twist our statements because they know they can't win against the truth. Disgraceful, really.

So having stirred people up, Stephen was caught and brought before the council where more people were brought in to lie against him. Chapter seven of the book of Acts tells us Stephen's response after the high priest questioned Stephen whether these accusations were true.

I have always found it interesting that Stephen starts his defense by going way back with Abram and tells the story of the Hebrew people. A story that all the crowd listening knew. The crowd was with him until he boldly called them stiff-necked and uncircumcised in their hearts and ears, and that they always resisted the Holy Ghost as their fathers did.

Hearing this charge, they were angered, grabbed Stephen, and literally began to bite him with their teeth. Even under attack Stephen, being full of the Holy Ghost, looked toward heaven and saw the heavens open. This was just too much for the ungodly crowd as they covered their ears so as not to hear anything else Stephen had to say.

There are times people do not want to hear what we have to say about our experience with Jesus, but we must testify concerning the things the Lord has done for us. We may meet that one who is seeking eternal life, and we have the answer.

Having put their hands on Stephen, they dragged him outside the city and stoned him to death.

This is what I want you to see about Stephen. This is when you know the person truly knows Jesus. As stones were being hurled at Stephen's head and body, he called upon God (Acts 7:59-60) saying, "Lord Jesus, receive my spirit." Stephen knew in just a matter of moments he was going to die. He did not wrestle with the thought. He did not attempt to bargain his way for more time. He simply wanted to make sure the Lord would receive him.

We have no idea when our time in this flesh will be done. I believe it would be safe to say most of us have lost a loved one suddenly, without warning and without the opportunity to say goodbye. This alerts us to the importance of knowing Jesus fully every day, for we do not know when He will call us home. It's a beautiful testament that Stephen was ready and while knowing his passing was imminent, he commended himself into the hands of Jesus.

Perhaps even more astonishing were Stephen's last words. "Lord, lay not this sin to their charge." If we are not at a place in our heart that we could pray that prayer for the people taking our life, then we don't know Jesus the way we think we do. Ouch, I know, but think about it. If we "know Him" the way Stephen knew Him, then we would be able to forgive even our murderers. As Jesus prayed "Father forgive them for they know not what they do," Stephen was so full of the Holy Ghost, he was able to pray the same prayer.

If you need a gauge to measure how well you know Him, or how full of the Holy Ghost you are, this is a tell-tale sign. We don't really know Him until we can forgive those who spitefully use us, hurt us, or seek to destroy us.

Stephen's position and ministry in the church was short, but how powerful and effective it was.

> "But I say unto you, love your enemies, bless them who curse you, do good to them that hate you, and pray for them which despitefully use you, and persecute you."
>
> Jesus
>
> Matthew 5:44

Chapter Four

John, the Apostle

(Also called the Disciple whom Jesus Loved)

Just as Peter and Andrew were called away from their fishing nets to follow Jesus, so were James, and his brother John. Matthew (Matthew 4:18-22) and Mark (Mark 1:16-20) both tell the story of a day Jesus was walking along the shore of the sea of Galilee, when He came upon Peter and Andrew in their boat casting a net. After calling them to follow Him, which they did, Jesus walked along the shore a bit further and came upon James and John in their boat mending their nets along with their father Zebedee and some hired servants. Jesus called after James and John to follow Him. The brothers immediately dropped their nets and followed Jesus, leaving their father behind. The gospel account of this encounter doesn't tell us how Zebedee felt about being left by his two sons to continue the work of that particular day without them, but I personally would have liked to have known.

It didn't take long before John was being exposed to who Jesus really was. Not long after leaving his boat and his father behind, he would witness a man with an unclean spirit in the synagogue be delivered, hear teaching and preaching on the gospel of the kingdom, see Peter's mother in-law healed of a high fever, people possessed with devils delivered, and a throng from the surrounding towns seeking Jesus.

John was compelled several years later to write a book concerning Jesus, which we know as the gospel according to John. In his writings he wanted us to know exactly who Jesus was.

> In the beginning was the Word, and the Word was with God, and the Word was God. The same was in the beginning with God. All things were made by him; and without him was not anything made that was made. In him was life; and the life was the light of men. And the light shineth in darkness; and the darkness comprehended it not … And the Word was made flesh, and dwelt among us, (and we beheld his glory, the glory as of the only begotten of the Father) full of grace and truth.
>
> John 1:1-5,14

Apostle John completely understood the deity of Jesus. It's threaded throughout his gospel, and he wanted us to understand as well.

John described Jesus as the Word, that Word which spoke the very existence of everything that had been created. He wrote of Nicodemus, who heard the gospel message spoken by Christ himself of the command of being born again. He recorded the story of the woman of Samaria who believed and through her many in Samaria believed. John also wrote of witnessing the healing of the blind man who had been born blind. He reinforced Christ's testimony of truth as Jesus said, "He dwelleth with you and shall be IN you" (John14:17), knowing that Jesus spoke of the infilling of the Holy Ghost that would come. Yes, John knew exactly who Jesus was.

John also referred to himself as the "disciple whom Jesus loved." John used this phrase five times in his gospel in reference to himself. John the apostle may not have been as demonstrative as Peter, not as outgoing or extroverted, but John was deep. He had love in his heart for Jesus and he knew Jesus loved him deeply as well. It's no surprise when John wrote his letters later in ministry, that he would write about the love of God. Jesus stated this as a prerequisite to keeping His commandments. John recorded the words of Jesus in his gospel.

> If ye love me, keep my commandments.
>
> John 14:15

This is also another great measuring stick to tell how well you live for the Lord. If you love Him, you will keep His commandments. If you keep His commandments, it shows your love for Him. Conversely, if you do not keep His commandments, it's a sign showing you don't love Him as you should or could. We've all heard the old adage, "to know him is to love him." There's much truth about this saying. Not only in the natural sense, but in the religious sense as well. It suggests that the more you become familiar with someone, and understand their ways and who they truly are, your appreciation and love for them will grow. This is also true in getting to know Jesus. The more you pray, study His word, learn His nature, you will build a greater appreciation and love for Him. As a result of that love, you will obey Him and keep His commandments.

In his epistles, John continues to write concerning the love of God and reinforce the fact that he knew exactly who Jesus is: The Christ, the Son of God.

> Whosoever believeth that Jesus is the Christ is born of God: and everyone that loveth him that begat loveth him also that is begotten of him. By this we know that we love the children of God, when we love God, and keep his commandments. For this is the love of God, that we keep his commandments: and his commandments are not grievous.
>
> I John 5:1-3

By spending time with Jesus, John knew the nature of Christ. One of deity, one of power and one of love.

It was John the apostle who, while standing near the cross as Jesus was hanging and being crucified, received direction. Jesus looking down and seeing Mary his mother, his mother's sister, Mary the wife of Cleophas, and Mary Magdalene. Jesus said to Mary his mother, "Woman, behold thy son. Then he said to John, Behold thy mother. From that hour forward John took Mary into his own home and cared for her" (John 19:26-27).

Under the wicked rule of the Roman Emperor Domitian, John was forcefully exiled to the Greek isle of Patmos. This was a secluded place Roman leaders used to rid themselves of those whom they viewed as political and religious dissidents. For John, this was punishment for his testimony of Christ and his teachings.

John, apparently well into his nineties, now found himself isolated from the churches and brethren he had served for many years. No doubt, Domitian thought this would put a stop to John and his preaching of Christ. Little did the emperor know that John continued to serve his Savior on Patmos just as faithfully as he had in Jerusalem.

> I was in the Spirit on the Lord's Day, and heard behind me a great voice, as of a trumpet, saying, "I am Alpha and Omega, the first and the last: and, what thou seest, write in a book, and send it unto the seven churches which are in Asia; unto Ephesus, and unto Smyrna, and unto Pergamos, and unto Thyatira, and unto Sardis, and unto Philadelphia, and unto Laodicea." And I turned to see the voice that spake with me. And being turned, I saw seven golden candlesticks; and in the midst of the seven candlesticks one like unto the Son of man, clothed with a garment down to the foot, and girt about the paps with a golden girdle. His head and his hairs were white like wool, as white as snow; and his eyes were as a flame of fire; and his feet like unto fine brass, as if they burned in a furnace; and his voice as the sound of many waters. And he had in his

> right hand seven stars: and out of his mouth went a sharp two-edged sword: and his countenance was as the sun shineth in his strength. And when I saw him, I fell at his feet as dead. And he laid his right hand upon me, saying unto me, "Fear not; I am the first and the last; I am he that liveth, and was dead; and behold, I am alive for evermore."
>
> Revelation 1:10-18

This account speaks of the first time John has seen Jesus face to face since Jesus ascended into the heavens from Mt Olivet decades earlier. John was a young fisherman who worked with his brother and his father when Jesus called him. John, now an old man, exiled from civilization is about to write one of the greatest of prophecies known to humanity. And not just one prophecy, but a book foretelling the end of earth and time. Jesus the Savior of the world only entrusts these details to one who knows Him intimately.

As John began to write, he saw the heavens opened, sealed books unsealed, trumpets, angels, war in heaven, war on land and sea, visions of judgment, visions of doom, an harlot thrown into the pit, mankind judged, and those who have washed their robes white, rewarded with the New Jerusalem.

What do you think that young, modest fisherman would have said if he had known his walk with Jesus was going to bring him here? We are not all preachers, evangelists, teachers, pastors or prophets, but we can all know Jesus intimately, and that is what He desires for us.

> In this was manifested the love of God toward us, because that God sent his only begotten Son into the world, that we might live through him.
>
> I John 4:9

Chapter Five

A Woman in the City

(Also called "a sinner," "forgiven")

Luke, in his gospel, tells the story of a Pharisee named Simon, who desired Jesus to come to his house for supper. If you are not familiar with this beautiful story, I encourage you to read it before continuing this chapter. It can be found in Luke 7, verses 36 through 49.

Jesus entered Simon the Pharisee's house, with others joining them. Sitting down to eat, Luke tells us, "A woman of the city, which was a sinner," heard that Jesus was at the pharisee's house. She brought an alabaster box of ointment and somehow entered the house. I've always found this part of the story quite amazing. Apparently, this unnamed sinner woman simply entered Simon's house uninvited, knowing Jesus was there.

Once inside, she stood behind Jesus and began to weep. She proceeded to kneel, washing the feet of Jesus with her tears, and soon was wiping his feet with her hair to dry them. With his feet dry, she began to kiss his feet and brought out the ointment and began to anoint the feet of Jesus.

How embarrassing and humiliating this would be for most people, but as we read the story, we begin to realize what a mess this woman must have made of her life. So much so that she set aside any pride to seek forgiveness. Rather than run from Jesus carrying the weight of her sin, after hearing Jesus was in Simon's house, she ran to Him. This is what happens many times when someone has hit the bottom and they learn what they need is Jesus.

I remember a Sunday morning, several years ago, after the congregation sang a couple worship songs, I began to teach the adult Sunday school class. My class introduction was interrupted by a young man who had spent years as a drug addict. Someone had invited him to church, and this was his second or third time in attendance. So moved by the singing, worship, and movement of the Holy Ghost, he walked to the altar area, lifted his hands high, and began to pray. We stopped what we were doing and several of the church members gathered around to pray for him and with him. I was so touched that day as that young man repented of his sins and gave his heart to the Lord. Through his repentance he proclaimed very loudly, "I'll never go back, I'll never go back!" He was speaking of the drug life he was leaving behind. That was the same desperation the sinner lady from the city must have felt the day she interrupted Jesus' dinner with Simon.

As Simon the Pharisee watched all that was happening, he was appalled. "If Jesus was really a prophet, he would know this woman was a sinner." Jesus spoke up, "Simon, I have somewhat to say unto thee." A lesson was about to be taught.

Jesus quizzed Simon about forgiveness, sharing a story with him. The point being made that whom little is forgiven, the same loves little. But those who are forgiven of many sins love much.

As Jesus continued to explain things to Simon, the "woman from the city, which was a sinner" did not stop kissing the feet of Jesus or anointing His feet with ointment.

The final words of Jesus concerning the matter was to the woman. "Thy sins are forgiven. Thy faith hath saved thee; go in peace."

True repentance leads to deep desire and complete forgiveness inspires immense love.

In my years of ministry, I have seen many people come to the Lord. Some who were raised in church and were always in the presence of apostolic Pentecostal preaching and teaching, and some who grew up never having any type of relationship with the Lord until finding it in adulthood. I have observed those who came to know Jesus later in life, not having a church background, many times had a deeper appreciation and love for the Lord because they were lost and realized they were lost and Jesus found them. They had found forgiveness, covering many sins.

Unfortunately, some who are raised in the church gain a sense of entitlement which can be spiritually destructive. We must always remember that none of us are worthy. Salvation is never earned because of our heritage. We all, whether we are raised in church or struggle in the world into adulthood, come to Jesus the same way. Repentance, baptism in Jesus' name and the infilling of the Holy Ghost.

You see, Simon the Pharisee had a sense of entitlement. It did not serve him well. But the woman from the city realized she was just a sinner who needed Jesus. The way she came to Jesus certainly was not dignified, but it accomplished what she needed. She found mercy and forgiveness.

Let us never forget what Jesus has done for us in the past. Never forget the times you or your children were healed by Jesus. What is healing worth? What is salvation worth? Sometimes in our frustrations with life, it can be easy to forget what the Lord has done for us or our families. Occasionally, we need to simply throw ourselves down at Jesus' feet and worship.

I don't know what became of the unnamed woman from the city after that day. I would like to believe the experience with Jesus, in the dining room of Simon's house, was forever life-changing, but Luke doesn't tell us. But this one thing I do know of that day, that one special day, that woman found everything she needed.

"If the Son therefore shall make you free, ye shall be free indeed."

Jesus

John 8:36

Chapter Six
Bartimaeus
(Also called: Son of Timaeus and "a certain blind man")

Luke tells the story of a "certain blind man" who was sitting on the roadside in Jericho begging when he heard a commotion coming his way. In his gospel, Mark tells us the blind man was Bartimaeus, the son of Timaeus. This happens to be one of my many favorites in the Word of God. I love this story so much because I see something in Bartimaeus that I love to see in people today when they approach Jesus.

The blind man heard a great noise down the road, but being blind, he had to rely on others to explain what was happening. They told him Jesus was walking toward them, and a great crowd of people were with Him and apparently pressing in on Him. Having heard of Jesus and His healings and miracles, Bartimaeus saw this as a grand opportunity to be healed.

Hearing the crowd, but not knowing exactly where Jesus was, he began to call out, "Jesus, thou son of David, have mercy on me." Repeatedly, he called out, hoping that amid the noisy throng, Jesus would hear him. Those standing nearby, and the others leading the crowd of people along the road, found the screaming of Bartimaeus to be rather annoying. They insisted that he stop all the yelling and stop drawing attention to himself, which only made the blind man yell out even louder.

"Jesus, thou son of David, have mercy on me!!!"

Those nearby, exhorting Bartimaeus to shut up, remind me of people today who tell us that all the hand raising, outward praising, and worshipping are unnecessary. It simply reveals they have not had the experience with Jesus that they need. When you have been in the darkness for so long, be it physical or spiritual, you cannot help but praise loudly and openly when you have been delivered. This was the blind man's opportunity, and he wasn't going to miss it. He was positioned for the miraculous.

As Jesus, and all the people pressing in moved forward, He heard the now screaming voice of Bartimaeus, "Jesus, thou son of David, have mercy on me," which caused Jesus to stop. Looking toward the side of the road, where the throng continued, Jesus saw him.

Commanding that the blind man be brought to Him, the people standing near Bartimaeus finally encouraged him. "Be of good comfort, rise; He's calling you." Throwing off his coat, he made his way to Jesus.

It's interesting to note that Jesus, seeing Bartimaeus, could have simply walked over to him, but instead, commanded that Bartimaeus come to Him. I hear so many people get bogged down on how much effort one must do to find Jesus. If salvation is truly free, there's nothing for me to do, they say. This has done nothing but produce cheap grace. Some stand on shaky ground believing that in the end, Jesus will save them because He's full of love and grace. I believe the correct attitude would be for us to be willing to do anything to know Christ. If knowing Him is worth it, then let's put some effort into it, what do you say?

Bartimaeus just spent some time screaming out for the attention of Jesus. He wasn't about to get caught up in who is really putting in the most effort here. He has been called by Jesus, and he wasn't going to waste time and lose what he has been seeking.

"What wilt thou that I should do unto thee?" I have often said this was a glorious time for Bartimaeus. At this very moment he could have asked Jesus for absolutely anything. I'm not saying Jesus would have given him certain requests but notice that Jesus opened the door completely with His question.

Some believe Jesus asked Bartimaeus the question to force him to answer out loud whatever his request might be, so everyone in the crowd could hear and know. Some say Jesus wanted Bartimaeus to vocalize his faith and desire. Perhaps that's true, but it didn't take the blind man long to decide what his most urgent need was. "Lord, that I might receive my sight."

What a beautiful opportunity Bartimaeus had been presented with. To stand face to face with the Savior and Healer and ask for whatever he desired. We have that opportunity every day.

Jesus healed him of his blindness, restoring his sight, informing him that it was his faith that saved him. Then Bartimaeus did something spectacular. Mark wrote that Bartimaeus "followed Jesus in the way."

Perhaps the desire to be healed of his blindness is what prompted Bartimaeus to call out for Jesus, but when everything was said and done, it had grown into a desire to know Him. As we find forgiveness, healing, or salvation, it should grow something inside of us that makes us desire our Savior more.

> "The Spirit of the Lord is upon me, because he hath anointed me to preach the gospel to the poor; He hath sent me to heal the brokenhearted, to preach deliverance to the captives, and recovering of sight to the blind, to set at liberty them that are bruised, to preach the acceptable year of the Lord."
>
> Jesus
>
> Luke 4:18-19

Chapter Seven

Mary Magdalene

(Also called "the Other Mary")

We find the first mention of Mary Magdalene in Luke's gospel when he is giving us the list of those traveling with Jesus through cities and villages, "preaching and showing the glad tidings of the kingdom of God." The twelve apostles are with Jesus, as are several women. Luke explains that these women ministered to Jesus of their substance. They provided financial and material support for the ministry out of their own resources.

In addition to giving the names of these women, Luke also gives a little detail concerning Mary's past, writing, "and certain women, which had been healed of evil spirits and infirmities, Mary called Magdalene, out of whom went seven devils" (Luke 8:2).

I'm not sure how Mary felt when she found out later that Luke had included this detail concerning her past in his letter to Theophilus. There seems to be a part of everyone's past that we're not thrilled about being broadcast. However, this gives us a small insight into Mary's past and helps us understand why she followed Jesus and loved Him so.

When a person has been deep in sin and they come to know Jesus, His forgiveness and love, how can they not love Him and deeply appreciate what He has done. We don't know the circumstances surrounding Mary, or why she was possessed of devils, but when she encountered Jesus, her life obviously changed.

She completely committed herself to Jesus and His ministry. So much so that, when Jesus traveled through cities and towns preaching and healing the sick, Mary was one of his greatest supporters. Imagine the miracles Mary witnessed while traveling with Jesus and the apostles.

When a person has been blessed and set free to the degree Mary was, it will inspire you to be involved. It is life changing for one who finds freedom and deliverance from Jesus. They will tell everyone they know what Jesus has done. They'll want to be involved and right in the middle of what Jesus is doing for others. Mary no doubt felt the same way.

In addition to being appreciative for her deliverance and desiring to support the ministry of Jesus, Mary Magdalene apparently built a strong relationship with Mary the mother of Jesus. After more than three years of ministry and teaching, Jesus is taken by the High Priests, scribes and elders to be judged and crucified.

John the apostle tells the story in chapter 19 of his gospel concerning the crucifixion. The Roman soldiers placed a crown of thorns upon the head of Jesus, put a purple robe on him to mock his deity, and smote him with their hands. After nailing him to a wooden cross, they lifted him into the air. As Jesus struggled physically with breathing and surviving, he looked down at those watching and who were standing near the cross. There he saw Mary Magdalene, the woman of whom he had cast out seven devils. She followed him to the end.

> Now there stood by the cross of Jesus his mother, and his mother's sister, Mary the wife of Cleophas, and Mary Magdalene.
>
> John 19:25

When my first daughter was born, I was blessed to be in the delivery room to experience the birth. She was born at 1:58 on a sunny, cool autumn day. I remember hearing her whimpering cry as the doctor turned her one way and then another way, checking her out to make sure she was healthy. She was then handed off to a nurse who measured her, and weighed her, and put a little baby bracelet on her tiny wrist. The nurse then turned to me, reaching my newborn daughter toward me, and said "dad." I took that eight-pound, seven-ounce baby in my arms and could not believe all the emotions I was feeling. I bragged for years, and still do to this day, that I got to hold my baby before her momma did. There was just something special about it.

Now think about Mary Magdalene. Four years earlier she was a woman wracked in sin, and living a life that she probably was not very proud about. Then she met Jesus, who delivered her from devils that had her bound. For more than three years she had followed Jesus, supported his ministry, and became dear friends with Mary his mother. She was at the cross when Jesus died and gave up the ghost. Now three miserable days have passed, and she desires to anoint the body with sweet spices. Then Mark tells us something incredible.

> Now when Jesus was risen early the first day of the week, he appeared first to Mary Magdalene, out of whom he had cast seven devils.
>
> Mark 16:9

Can you imagine how Mary Magdalene must have felt? Can you imagine being the first one for Jesus to appear to following His resurrection? How special that must have been. I know the Bible tells us she, and the other women, were "affrighted," but think about later that day, when she was sitting in her home running the amazing day through her mind. Right about then it probably hit her. "I saw Him first, He resurrected from the dead, and I was the first one to see Him."

How special Mary must have felt.

Jesus was with the apostles, disciples, and the women for forty days teaching and preparing them for His ascension into heaven. Commanding them to return to Jerusalem until "they be endued" with power from the Holy Ghost. Luke, in the book of Acts, does not mention Mary Magdalene by name, when naming those in the upper room who were about to be filled with the Holy Ghost, but he did once again include "the women."

Mary Magdalene traveled a great distance in four short years. From being held captive by the wickedness of the devil, being delivered by Jesus, witnessing the tragedy of His death, to being the first to witness Him alive again. And then being with the apostles and other disciples, as the Holy Ghost fell upon every one of them in the upper room. What a ride!

If you desire a life like Mary's, chase after Jesus. Never be satisfied with where you are in Him. Always desire more. You may one day be incredibly overwhelmed with Jesus the way Mary was early in the morning on that first day of the week.

> My heart is fixed, O God, my heart is fixed: I will sing and give praise.
>
> Psalm 57:7

Chapter Eight

Nicodemus

(Also called, A Ruler of the Jews, A Pharisee)

We find a Pharisee, who apparently was highly regarded, seeking Jesus by night. John, the author of the gospel where this event is told, doesn't explain why Nicodemus sought this Rabbi by night, but I believe it is safe to presume it was to protect himself from criticism, since many of the scribes and pharisees did not believe on Jesus.

Nicodemus obviously believed on Jesus, for John quotes him as saying in John Chapter Three, "Rabbi, we know that thou art a teacher come from God, for no man can do these miracles that thou doest, except God be with him."

It was truly a wonderful thing that this Pharisee leader believed Jesus was come from God, but simply believing isn't enough. Jesus desired to teach him more so that Nicodemus could be saved.

Jesus told Nicodemus that if a man is not born again, he cannot see the kingdom of God. This statement completely confused Nicodemus, as he asked Jesus how it was even possible for a man to enter a second time into his mother's womb and be born.

Here's the thing. Jesus was talking of Spiritual things. Nicodemus was still stuck in the flesh.

May I put Nicodemus on the back burner for a moment and explain something that must happen if we are going to find our obsession with Jesus? You've got to stop thinking in human terms. The thoughts and ways of the Creator of the universe, and sacrificial Lamb of our salvation, are far above ours. I believe God has simplified most of heaven and earth in terms we can understand, but to know Jesus we must lay down our carnality and try to see what He sees. One of the ways we accomplish this is through prayer, which we will discuss in a later chapter.

Jesus, in his patient way, attempted to explain this to Nicodemus. "Except a man be born of water (baptism) and of the Spirit (Holy Ghost) he cannot enter into the kingdom of God. That which is born of flesh, is flesh. That which is born of Spirit is spirit."

In verses five and six of John chapter three, Jesus uses the Greek words "pneumatos" and "pneuma" respectively, which are translated into English for our benefit as Spirit. Notice the capital S, signifying not human spirit but Spirit of God. The words are versatile words that also mean "wind" or "breath." Interestingly, before Jesus ascended into heaven, he breathed on the disciples and commanded they receive the Holy Ghost. Then on the day of Pentecost, when the Holy Ghost fell upon the one hundred twenty, there came a sound from heaven as a rushing mighty wind.

Poor Nicodemus still didn't understand. "How can these things be?" he asked in verse nine. By verse ten it seems to me that Jesus was losing some of that heavenly patience. Are you a master of Israel and you don't know these things?

As Jesus continued to teach Nicodemus, the Lord spoke prophetically of His crucifixion and the necessity of believing on His Name. To me, it doesn't seem John completely finished the story. I would enjoy it more if John had said, Nicodemus believed on the new birth and lived happily ever after, but we're missing detail. However, Nicodemus does show up again in the scripture.

Later, in John Chapter Seven, at the time of the Feast of Tabernacles, which would have been in the Fall of the year, Jesus would find himself challenged by other pharisees. As Jesus spoke with them, some of the people believed, some questioned, and some wanted Jesus carried away and killed. It was Nicodemus, the Pharisee and ruler of the Jews, who spoke up in a way to protect Jesus, challenging the other pharisees, "Doth our law judge any man before it hears him and know what he doeth?" Nicodemus, to draw the crowd back away from Jesus reminded them that, according to the Law, one cannot be convicted or sentenced to death without hearing his defense. Without openly proclaiming to be a follower of Christ in the presence of his fellow pharisees, Nicodemus said just enough to defuse the situation against Jesus.

Now on the day that Jesus was crucified, when the solders came to break the legs of the three on the crosses, they discovered that Jesus had already died. The bodies needed to be laid in graves or tombs before dark, so John the apostle tells us in chapter nineteen of his gospel that Joseph of Arimathaea sought Pilate to allow him to take the body of Jesus for burial. Joseph was a disciple of Christ, but secretly, because he feared the Jews. There was another man who joined Joseph in this endeavor. This other man brought a mixture of myrrh and aloes of about one hundred pounds in weight. Together they carried the body of Jesus, wound it in linen clothes with the spices, according to the custom of the Jews to bury. They then laid Jesus in a new sepulchre which was in a garden. The other man, the one who brought the spices and helped Joseph was Nicodemus, the Pharisee.

Biblically the story of Nicodemus ends there. Luke, when he writes the book of Acts, does not mention Nicodcmus as one of the one hundred twenty in the upper room. No mention of him throughout the book of Acts, or any of the letters written later by the apostles.

I would like to think that a man who would seek Jesus out for private teachings, who would defend and protect him in the face of hypocritical, angry people at the end of a feast, and as an act of love would join with a friend to give the Lord a proper burial, had found his way. Although we cannot prove it, I somehow believe before Nicodemus drew his last breath, he found the new birth that Jesus had told him about.

> Therefore, if any man be in Christ, he is a new creature: old things are passed away, behold, all things are become new.
>
> II Corinthians 5:17

Chapter Nine
Philip, the Apostle

A fisherman from Bethsaida of Galilee before Jesus called him to follow Him, as recorded in the gospel of John Chapter One, Philip didn't appear to be one of the standout apostles like Peter, James and John, but what was written concerning Philip, certainly reveals a passion to introduce people to Jesus.

We first hear of Philip's call to follow Jesus while Jesus is traveling through Galilee and comes across Philip. "Follow me" was the words of the Messiah, and Philip did not hesitate. What Philip did next appears to be his main strength as a follower of Christ, which is to lead people to Jesus.

Philip went searching for his friend Nathanael (Bartholmew) and found him under a fig tree. "We have found him, of whom Moses in the law, and the prophets, did write, Jesus of Nazareth, the son of Joseph." You could say, Nathanael was the first of many Philip would bring to Christ.

Like Nathanael, Philip watched and listened for the next three and one-half years as Jesus healed the sick, raised the dead, opened blind eyes, and enjoyed victories over devils as Jesus gave the apostles power.

Not long before Jesus gave Himself to be crucified, He had ridden into Jerusalem upon the back of a donkey. There were Greeks in Jerusalem who had come to worship at the feast. Desiring to see Jesus, they came to Philip and asked if he would take them to Him. Philip, finding Andrew, went together to Jesus telling him of these strangers' request to see Him.

The following weeks would bring the crucifixion and resurrection of Jesus, His forty days of teaching and His ascension into heaven. The apostles and other believers would go back to Jerusalem and tarry until they were filled with power. As Luke penned the beginning of the book of Acts, he listed Philip as one of the approximately one hundred twenty in the upper room to receive the Holy Ghost, evidenced with speaking in tongues.

As a mighty church was growing in Jerusalem, the believers of Christ began to spread across the known world due to persecution. Stephen, a man full of faith and of the Holy Ghost had been stoned to death by an angry mob, others had been imprisoned, and a young man named Saul had acquired letters from the Chief Priests giving him the authority to arrest any who believed on Jesus.

During this time, Philip traveled to the city of Samaria to preach the gospel of Christ to those living there. As Philip preached and ministered to the people, he laid his hands on their sick and afflicted and prayed for them. Seeing demons cast out of people, and many who were lame walking, many of the people believed his message of Jesus. Philip was able to baptize them in the name of the Lord, both men and women.

Word spread to Peter and John in Jerusalem that Samaria was experiencing great revival. Together, they traveled to Samaria to help Philip. Upon arrival, Peter and John laid hands on those who had been baptized and many of them received the baptism of the Holy Ghost.

After having great revival in the city of Samaria, Peter and John continued to travel throughout the cities of the Samaritans preaching Christ. As for Philip, the Lord spoke to him specifically to travel toward Gaza, which was desert.

Let's examine this for a moment. One of the things I love about Philip was his desire to lead people to Jesus. We can see throughout his ministry a desire to witness and introduce people to Jesus who otherwise might not know Him. Now, the Lord is leading this great witness, who loves to win souls, to go to a desert area where the odds of him having a group to preach to are slim.

When we make Jesus our obsession, we will follow His guidance. We may not always understand why the Lord is leading us one way or another, but if we trust Him and follow His will, we will see His plan always has a purpose.

As Philip made his way into the desert of Gaza, he saw in the distance a chariot. Again, the Lord spoke to Philip and instructed him to join himself with this chariot. Philip began to run, and drawing near the chariot, he heard this Ethiopian man, who was a servant of Candace, queen of the Ethiopians reading.

"Do you understand what you are reading?" Philip enquired. "How can I, unless some man should guide me," the servant responded.

Stopping the chariot, he invited Philip to get on board. Philip, no doubt thankful the man stopped the chariot so he wouldn't have to continue running to keep up, climbed on.

Realizing that the servant was reading a prophecy written in the book of Isaiah concerning Jesus, Philip started at that place and preached Jesus to the Ethiopian servant. Before their conversation was finished, the Ethiopian servant commanded the chariot to be stopped again so Philip could baptize him. This is what happens when one is obsessed with Jesus and shares the testimony to everyone he meets. The Lord led Philip to a desert to win one soul.

After baptizing the Ethiopian servant, Philip found himself in Azotus, a city on the coast of the Mediterranean Sea where Luke writes that Philip continued to preach Christ in each of those cities, until he reached Caesarea, which totaled at least six cities.

I realize Philip was an apostle and a preacher. It was his calling to teach and preach to the masses concerning Christ. One does not have to be a minister to minister. When one is obsessed with Jesus and secure in their salvation, there should be a desire within us to win others to Christ.

> The fruit of the righteous is a tree of life; and he that winneth souls is wise.
>
> Proverbs 11:30

Chapter Ten

Cornelius

(A Centurion, A devout Man)

Cornelius, in Caesarea, who was a centurion or officer of a band of soldiers called the Italian band, is covered in only one chapter of the Bible, but what a powerful chapter it is.

Luke described Cornelius in Acts Chapter Ten as a devout man, and one that feared God. With Cornelius being a Gentile, I'm not sure if he really understood at the time who God was. But whatever his understanding, Cornelius determined to fear, or reverence God.

He also gave much alms to the people, which in New Testament terms meant he gave a great deal of his own money to help the poor. He prayed to God always and taught his family to do the same. Cornelius desired in his heart to do what was right and honor God, whomever this God was.

One day, about three o'clock in the afternoon, God gave him a vision. An angel of the Lord came to him, and after the initial fearfulness that seems to always follow when someone sees an angel, the angel of the Lord said, "Cornelius, your prayers and helping the poor have come up to God as a memorial." The angel then instructed Cornelius to send men to Joppa to find a man named Peter (the apostle) and he "will tell you what you ought to do."

Without delay Cornelius sent two servants and a soldier on their way to Joppa to find Peter. As the men traveled on their journey, Peter, who was on the roof of Simon's house praying, received a vision from the Lord concerning the Lord cleansing the unclean (Gentiles) and telling him to go with these men, and do not question.

Days later, when Peter and the six Jewish brethren, who had traveled with him, reached the house of Cornelius, they found Cornelius had invited his relatives and close friends to hear what this man Peter had to say concerning God.

Peter explained that he was not a god, but a man just like them. And he stressed that it was unlawful for a Jew to enter the house of a Gentile, however he now understood the vision that he received on the house top, so he was happy to share with these Gentiles what the Lord had to say to them.

Peter opened his mouth and began to teach this house full of Gentiles. Peter at this time, did not realize or believe that God would fill Gentiles with the Holy Ghost.

Peter preached Jesus, beginning with the ministry and miracles, and Peter proclaimed to be a witness to these things. He preached the resurrection of Christ and testified that Jesus is the judge, and that all should believe on the name of Jesus and receive remission of sins.

Luke writes that while Peter was still preaching, the Holy Ghost fell upon Cornelius and all those in his house, and they all began to speak in tongues and magnify God.

Peter and the men who were with him were amazed that also on the Gentiles God would pour out the Holy Ghost. Peter, the Bible says, knew they had received the Holy Ghost because he heard them speak in tongues (verses 45-46) so he commanded all of them to be baptized in the Name of the Lord.

Here's some takeaways I want to share with you concerning Cornelius. He apparently didn't even know exactly who God was, but he wanted to please Him. So, Cornelius lived a life to please God, and it showed his hunger for God. When God directed Cornelius, what to do to be saved, he followed through without hesitation. As Peter preached Jesus to him and his family and friends, his heart was open to receive. Then after receiving the Holy Ghost, he followed through with baptism.

Cornelius was hungry and ready to receive.

Cornelius was the first Gentile to receive the Holy Ghost after the day of Pentecost, proving to Peter and the other apostles that Jesus came to save all people from their sins.

If you are reading this and you love God, but you're not exactly sure who He is, or what He commands you to do, if you will reverence Him and live for Him in the way you know how, He will open to you what you need to do. He will guide you and direct you. I truly believe if we are sincerely desirous to know the One true God, He will reveal himself to us.

> "I indeed baptize you with water unto repentance, but he that cometh after me is mightier than I, whose shoes I am not worthy to bear, he shall baptize you with the Holy Ghost and with fire."
>
> John the Baptist
>
> Matthew 3:11

Chapter Eleven

Paul, the Apostle

(Also called Saul, Saul of Tarsus)

The first mention of Apostle Paul was in the Seventh Chapter of Acts, before his conversion when he was still called Saul. Even though the event of Stephen's death was tragic and nothing to celebrate, I've always felt the way Luke introduced Saul to the story was quite poetic.

> Then they cried out with a loud voice, and stopped their ears, and ran upon him with one accord, and cast him out of the city, and stoned him and the witnesses laid down their clothes at a young man's feet, whose name was Saul.
>
> Acts 7:58

For someone who might be reading the book of Acts for the first time, they would not realize what an impact this young man would eventually have in the kingdom of God. On this particular day, he did not participate in the stoning of Stephen, but he consented to his death, and no doubt thought these ungodly men were doing the Lord's work.

Saul, a Pharisee, was a highly intelligent young man who had studied under the teaching of one, Gamaliel, a Pharisee himself and a teacher of Jewish law and a member of the Sanhedrin, which was the supreme religious and judicial council of the Jewish people. Saul was not a slacker, nor uneducated, but held impressive credentials by being associated with Gamaliel.

Saul was driven by a zeal for Jewish traditions (Galatians 1:13-14) and ignorance in unbelief (I Timothy 1:13). He ruthlessly and violently persecuted the church, searched houses in Jerusalem and other areas of Israel, and upon finding believers of Jesus, had them arrested and thrown into prison.

The story of Saul's conversion is written by Luke in Acts Chapter Nine. I want to take my time to show you several things in this chapter that I've always found quite amazing. Saul breathed out "threatenings and slaughter" against the followers of Jesus. He asked for letters from the high priest which gave him authority to travel to Damascus to actively seek followers of Christ. Upon finding any who believed on Jesus, he had authority to arrest, bind and bring them back to Jerusalem.

While drawing near to the city, a light shined from heaven, and a voice called out to Saul, "Saul, Saul, why persecutest thou me?" I want you to pay attention to Saul's response.

"Who art thou Lord?" Saul did not know Jesus, but he realized the voice that was speaking to him was greater than man. Saul heard a voice of authority and deity.

After the Lord identified himself and instructed Saul what to do, Saul, trembling and blind completed his trip to Damacus.

Not long after, the Lord spoke to a believer of Christ named Ananais, instructing him to go to the street called Straight, to the house of a man called Judas, and ask for Saul of Tarsus. Ananais did have some hesitation, knowing the reputation and hatred of Saul. But Ananais, having been assured by the Lord that Saul was praying for direction and that he was a chosen vessel, to bear the name of Jesus before the Gentiles, kings, and the children of Israel, entered the house. Then something beautiful happened. Ananais laid his hands on Saul of

Tarsus and called him brother.

> Brother Saul, the Lord, even Jesus, that appeared unto thee in the way as thou camest, hath sent me, that thou mightest receive thy sight and be filled with the Holy Ghost.
>
> Acts 9:17

Luke tells us, the scales on Saul's eyes fell off allowing him to see; he rose up and was baptized and, after eating, received strength. Luke also tells us that Saul immediately began to preach Jesus in the synagogues and proved Christ, confounding the Jews.

Later, while at Antioch, (Acts 12) Saul, who at this time was also called Paul, was with certain prophets and teachers, and the Lord spoke that Saul and Barnabus should separate themselves and journey, preaching the gospel. After prayer and fasting, the group laid hands on the pair, praying for them, and sent them on what would become Apostle Paul's first missionary journey.

As Paul and Barnabus traveled, they visited at least seven cities preaching the gospel and establishing churches. They preached in synagogues and other areas proclaiming Jesus to be the Christ. Having great success, they were able to anoint elders in various cities to carry on the work as they continued their journeys.

It was in the city of Lystra where they came upon their greatest opposition. While preaching the Word in the city, Paul happened upon a man who had been lame since birth. While speaking, Paul perceived the man had faith to be healed. Paul commanded the man, "stand upright on thy feet." With that command, thc man stood and began leaping and walking.

Many of the people of the city falsely thought Paul and Barnabus must be gods. It grieved the two apostles that the people thought these things, and they told them they were men just like them.

During this time, men from the cities of Antioch and Iconium, where

Paul and Barnabus had preached, who opposed the apostles entered Lystra and persuaded some against the apostles. They stoned Paul into unconsciousness and threw his body outside of the city. The brethren who were with Paul thought he was dead as he lay on the street outside of the city. Slowly, Paul regained consciousness and was helped to his feet. Going back into the city of Lystra, Paul rested overnight and the next morning continued to Derbe preaching the gospel of Jesus Christ.

Can you imagine what Paul must have looked like and felt like the next day as he traveled with Barnabus on to Derbe? He probably had cuts and bruises about his head and face. He probably experienced a great deal of pain and soreness as he moved and walked. He had been stoned so brutally that he became unresponsive. His brethren thought he had died. Yet he rose up the very next morning, traveled to the next town and continued to preach the gospel of Jesus Christ.

Before ending their missionary journey, they returned to Lystra, Iconium and Antioch, preached the Word, and checked on the churches that they had founded by winning people to Christ. While there, they appointed elders in every church and exhorted them to continue in the faith.

Afterward, Paul and Barnabus spent much time in the city of Antioch, preaching and teaching with the brethren there and the church.

Later, Paul desired a second missionary journey to check on the churches that had been established, and so he took Silas with him, a prophet, recommended by the brethren. They traveled, confirming the churches and preaching the gospel.

It's interesting to note that the descriptive writing of the book of Acts by Luke during the second missionary journey, changed from "they" to "we" indicating he, Luke, traveled with Paul and Silas, as did others.

It is during this journey that Paul and Silas were locked away in prison, when they began to sing and worship the Lord at midnight.

Suddenly, Luke writes, there was a great earthquake, and the foundations of the prison were shaken, and the jail doors opened, and every prisoner's bands, or chains were loosed. This was terrible news for a jailer in those days. If any prisoners escaped during your watch, you were executed.

Paul reassured the jailer that all the prisoners were present, and none sought to escape. So moved was the jailer that he asked Paul and Silas what he needed to do to be saved. As Paul and Silas taught salvation to this man, he took them to his house, washed their stripes, for they had been beaten, and fed them. Before sunrise, the jailer and his entire family had heard the gospel, and had been baptized, believing on the Lord.

These types of miraculous conversions do not happen to a halfhearted "Christian" who does not pray or seek opportunity to win others to Christ. If we are going to be soul winners, we must be prayerful and ready, even if we are sitting in a prison, chained to the wall. This event is an example of Paul being so consumed with Jesus, it was his obsession.

While on their journey, it was at Thessalonica that Paul, Silas, and those brethren that traveled with them, were referred to as "those that have turned the world upside down." The evil men who made that charge against them meant it as an insult, but what a compliment that was for the people of God who traveled, teaching and preaching the Word of God. I'll take an insult like that any day.

While in Corinth on this journey, the Lord spoke to Paul in a dream and instructed him to not be afraid, but to preach the Word with boldness, for He, the Lord, had many people in that city. Being instructed of the Lord, Paul remained in Corinth for eighteen months, preaching and building a congregation.

During Paul's second missionary journey, he visited as many as fifteen cities, preaching the gospel, winning people to Christ, baptizing in Jesus Name, and establishing many churches.

As Paul began his third missionary journey, he came to Ephesus and met twelve men who seemed to be disciples. Paul, expecting that they had fully come to know Jesus in baptism and in the infilling of the Holy Ghost asked, (Acts 19:2) "Have ye received the Holy Ghost since ye believed?"

Surprised, the men confessed that they had not even heard of the Holy Ghost. Paul inquired more deeply, "Then how were you baptized?" These men were baptized by John the Baptist, as John baptized "unto repentance," stating that his followers, that is, John's followers should follow the One coming after him, which Paul explained to these men was Jesus.

These men, desiring to know God and be saved, were re-baptized in the Name of Jesus. Luke explains that when these men were baptized, Paul laid his hands on them and every one of them received the baptism of the Holy Ghost and began to speak in tongues.

Again, here is an example of a glorious event that is not going to happen to the halfhearted Christian who does not pray and is not sensitive to the Holy Ghost. Paul, who was obsessed with knowing Jesus and reaching the lost, met twelve men who were hungry for everything God had for them. Hunger for God is important. Let us be hungry.

After Paul's experience with these twelve men, he proceeded throughout Asia for a space of two years, so that all the people which dwelt in Asia heard the Word of the Lord, both Jews and Gentiles.

During this time, many miracles were brought about by the hands of Paul. So much so that from his body were brought handkerchiefs or aprons to the sick, and diseases and evil spirits left them. This was certainly a man who was obsessed with Jesus, knew Him well, and had the power of God to perform miracles.

On Apostle Paul's third missionary journey, there are fifteen cities mentioned that he visited, and the regions of Galatia and Phrygia.

Upon completion of his third missionary journey, Paul traveled to Caesarea where he entered the house of Philip the evangelist, not to be confused with Philip the Apostle. Philip the evangelist was one of the seven brethren appointed to care for the widows, along with Stephen and others, noted in Acts Chapter Six.

Luke tells us that he, Paul, and others stayed with Philip in his house for "many" days. It was during this visit that a prophet named Agabus prophesied that if Paul went to Jerusalem as planned, he would be put in chains. After the brethren with Paul tried mightily to convince him not to go to Jerusalem, Paul declared he was ready to be put in chains, and even put to death, for the name of Jesus, if that was to be. After much prayer, Paul, Luke and others traveled to Jerusalem as Paul had planned.

It did not take long for Paul to be accused of crimes he did not commit. Paul, in answering for himself angered those in opposition, and forty men took an oath that they would not eat anything until they had killed Paul the Apostle.

Being called a pestilent fellow, and a mover of sedition among all the Jews throughout the world, and a ringleader of the sect of the Nazarenes, who also profaned the temple, Paul sought to defend himself before Ananias the High Priest, and later Felix the Roman governor of Judea. Felix hoped for a bribe from Paul, but when none came forth and Felix saw that it pleased the Jews for Paul to be in prison, he left him there.

Before King Agrippa, Paul gave a testimony of his conversion which brought him to Jesus. How amazing it would be to stand before a king, governor or other powerful people and witness to them the things of God.

Finally, on a ship bound for Rome to appeal to Ceasar, even that seemed challenging. After anguishing through days of storms on the sea with two hundred, seventy-five others, the ship ran aground and broke apart. Paul and the others found themselves on the island of

Melita for months, where Paul continued to teach Christ and perform healings through the power of Jesus Name.

Once Paul arrived in Rome, he did exactly what we would expect him to do, knowing his obsession with sharing the good news of Jesus Christ. Luke tells us in closing out the book of Acts that many came to Paul's lodging where he expounded and testified the kingdom of God, persuading them concerning Jesus. He preached to this crowd from morning until the evening, where we are told some believed.

What an incredible testimony of a man who gave his entire life to know Jesus. Even while in chains and shipwrecked, he shared the gospel of Jesus Christ.

Apostle Paul, being driven to share the gospel of Jesus Christ, fulfilled three missionary journeys founding churches in dozens of cities. He wrote most of the New Testament, with many letters being written from prison while in chains. During Paul's ministry, he was beaten with thirty-nine stripes upon his back, five times. Three times beaten with rods. Once he was stoned and left outside the city for dead. Three times he suffered shipwreck. One night and one day he spent in the waters of the sea. In perils of robbers, the heathen, his own countrymen, and false brethren. He escaped multiple times from those who desired to kill him and spent at least six years in prisons for crimes which he did not commit.

If we ever begin to feel sorry for ourselves and feel persecuted, we should remember the testimony of Apostle Paul. A man who truly was obsessed with Jesus.

> "For I am now ready to be offered, and the time of my departure is at hand. I have fought a good fight, I have finished my course, I have kept the faith; henceforth there is laid up for me a crown of righteousness, which the Lord, the righteous judge shall give me at that day; and not to me only, but unto all them also that love his appearing."
>
> Apostle Paul in his second letter to Timothy
>
> II Timothy 4:6-8

Section Two
Practical Applications

Chapter Twelve

Prayer

A few years ago, I visited some friends in another state, and on Sunday I attended church with them. It's a rather large Apostolic Pentecostal congregation and the pastor is widely known. During his message this particular morning he began to talk about prayer. Somewhere along the way, he stated that prayer is hard. My initial reaction was one of shock. I was surprised that an Apostolic Pentecostal pastor would say to his congregation that prayer is hard.

As we left church to get lunch and I eventually said my goodbyes to return home, I thought heavily on his statement. I concluded that he was correct; that prayer certainly can be difficult at times, but I'm not sure I ever admitted it out loud up to this point. To be honest with you, his statement that day gave me a new perspective on prayer.

So let us go ahead and identify the elephant in the room. Yes, prayer can be difficult. Not because of the God to whom we pray, but rather our flesh, and the distractions of life.

If we are going to live as the apostles lived, with the power of the Holy Ghost, prayer must be our most important discipline, and that is exactly what prayer is, a discipline. We discipline ourselves to live our lives in an orderly adult manner. We discipline ourselves to bathe daily, and to go to work every day and be on time. We discipline ourselves to pay our bills on time, so our utilities are not turned off, so we do not suffer a huge reconnection fee.

We discipline ourselves to take care of our automobiles by changing the oil on time and watching tire pressure, so our vehicles last as long as possible. We change the filter on our home air conditioning unit, so it won't strain in the summer when it's hot outside.

We teach our children discipline as well. We put them to bed each night early enough so they can wake up in the morning and get to school on time. We teach them to discipline themselves, so they brush their teeth each day to avoid cavities and other oral health issues.

Prayer, although a spiritual matter rather than a natural matter, must be disciplined as well. It is much too easy to jump out of bed, get the kids ready for school, hurry out the door and find ourselves halfway through the day before we even think of prayer. For prayer to be effective, it must be an everyday discipline.

With prayer, you are seeking consistency. Pray each and every day, even if it's simply fifteen minutes a day. Don't go all week without prayer and then try to pray for ninety minutes on Sunday morning attempting to prepare your spirit for church. I'm not saying fifteen minutes is enough each day; consistency is key. When we go days without prayer, our spirit becomes weak and we are more susceptible to falling into temptation. Satan, our enemy, looks for weak spots in our life to take advantage of us.

Daily prayer leads us to open communication with Jesus. When we speak to Him as we do our closest friends, we will find He will begin to speak back to us and lead us in our daily walk. I have found personally, the more I pray and speak to Him, the more He speaks to me. Not only during times of prayer, but throughout the day as well. He is more likely to lead you to someone in need if you have prayed and are sensitive to His direction.

Daily prayer will give you a sense of continual prayer. An attitude of prayer, if you will. At least nine times in the book of Acts it is said that the speaker, whether it was an apostle or another disciple, spoke with boldness, or authority. When you have been communicating with Jesus, you will witness with boldness. I realize our own personalities can play a role in how bold we come across. I am quite the extrovert, and I have reached an age where I don't really care too much about what people think of me, so I don't hesitate to tell someone about Jesus if the opportunity arises. I understand someone who is quiet by nature, or an introvert may struggle more with witnessing, but daily prayer will indeed give you more boldness to speak out about what the Lord has done for you.

Daily prayer will lead you into the Spirit, which will give you strength to overcome weaknesses or temptations that you fight against. One of the uses of prayer is to strengthen your spirit in the Holy Ghost to overcome your flesh. It is difficult to break down strongholds without prayer. We do not fight against flesh and blood, but principalities and powers, and rulers of darkness. Our fight is a spiritual one, and we cannot be victorious without prayer.

When we enter into prayer, the deeper we go, the deeper we enter into the very nature of God. Prayer will take us into a dimension in God that the world cannot see or understand. It is a place our flesh can never take us. It is only through prayer.

If you have a desire to live with a Jesus obsession, you must have an encounter with Him that only comes through prayer. In the life of an overcomer, prayer is not an option.

When we pray, it is not only to strengthen us, but it is to help others as well. We pray intercessory prayers, we pray for our children, our pastor and our church. Prayer widens your scope of influence. Through prayer, and the power of the Holy Ghost, you may have a word or some help for someone you meet that day that the Lord led you to. I believe many times we are an encouragement to people and we never know.

It is important to stop life when we pray. Often, we can be guilty of praying as we run out the door to start our day, or we pray as we race to an appointment and hope it's enough. I have found, while it's wonderful to call on the Lord anytime day or night, my most effective prayers come when I stop life, shut myself in my prayer room, and concentrate on Him without distractions. It is during those times I can concentrate on Him and He on me, one on one. Even Jesus, when He prayed, would remove Himself from the crowds and go to the mountain or the garden alone to pray.

If it helps you to have a prayer list written out on paper or on a device, by all means use it. I don't think it bothers the Lord at all if we are praying our requests by memory or looking at a piece of paper. He just wants us to talk to Him. Be honest in your prayers and say what you need to say.

When my daughters were still at home, I would tell them they could say anything they needed to say to me, no matter what it was, as long as they said it respectfully. I believe our heavenly Father feels the same way. There have been times I have told the Lord I didn't understand a certain thing, or there have been times I told Him I was rather upset with a particular situation. I believe the Lord wants us to express our heart to Him. He's our heavenly Father, and He loves us. But remember, when we express ourselves to Him, He may speak a word back to us. Be humble and ready to receive.

The last bit of advice I would like to say concerning prayer is to keep the distractions out of your life as much as possible. You've no doubt heard the saying, "garbage in, garbage out." The Word of God teaches us:

> Finally, brethren, whatsoever things are true, whatsoever things are honest, whatsoever things are just, whatsoever things are pure, whatsoever things are lovely, whatsoever things are of good report, if there be any virtue, and if there be any praise, think on these things.
>
> Philippians 4:8

As you pray each day, be careful not to allow so much of the world inside your mind that it tears down what you have built in prayer.

"But thou, when thou prayest, enter into thy closet, and when thou hast shut thy door, pray to thy Father which is in secret, and thy Father which seeth in secret shall reward thee openly."

Jesus

Matthew 6:6

Chapter Thirteen
Fasting

Fasting, like prayer, is a discipline. I can't say that I have ever enjoyed fasting, but when a time of fasting is over, you feel a sense of victory. Fasting is to the body, what prayer is to the spirit. Just as we pray to keep our spirit under subjection, we fast to keep our bodies under subjection.

Apostle Paul tells us in I Corinthians that our bodies are the temple of the Holy Ghost, and we should not defile that temple. As part of that consecration, we are to be temperate in eating, drinking, and the care of our bodies. To overeat or have no restraint would be to abuse our bodies and therefore abuse the temple of God. Paul instructs us in Romans Chapter Twelve to "Present your bodies a living sacrifice, holy, acceptable unto God which is your reasonable service."

We enjoy feeding our flesh and caring for it. Many give their flesh anything it desires, but over time they realize the thing they have indulged in has now become a health concern or some other type of problem. One of the purposes of fasting is to keep a check on our flesh so that it does not control us, but rather we control it.

There are many ways to fast and many types of fasting. Usually when we think of fasting, we think of not eating food, but we can fast anything that we feel is attempting to control us. Not everyone can stop eating food due to health concerns such as diabetes, or other conditions. There are ways that anyone who desires to keep their flesh under subjection can fast.

I have known people who have fasted coffee for a certain amount of time, or chocolate for a certain amount of time. One could eat one meal per day and fast the other hours of the day for a certain amount of time. I know one man who was a big sports fanatic who fasted sports for thirty days. For one month he did not check scores, standings, or any games. Now that might not be a challenge for you at all, but it was a difficult fast for him. I'm sure we all know someone who has gone on a social media fast.

The point of fasting is to make it a sacrifice. Make it hurt. When you take prayer, and add sacrificial fasting, it can take you to another dimension in Christ. Jesus will always honor sacrifice when it is done humbly.

I have found in my experience that I do not feel victorious while I am in the midst of a fast. It can be difficult and you may not feel well during the fast, but after it is accomplished, God blesses.

Fasting can also be used to appeal to God concerning a certain situation or need. Queen Esther fasted as an appeal for God to save her people. Nehemiah fasted before the rebuilding of the walls of Jerusalem. Daniel fasted for God to give him understanding. The Ninevites fasted as a repentance to escape destruction. Anna the prophetess, in Luke chapter seven, served God with fasting and prayers daily.

When you begin a fast, focus on your goal. Are you fasting to keep your body under subjection to your spirit? Maybe to grow stronger in your spirit in the Holy Ghost? Maybe you're fasting in unity and prayer for your church, or pastor, or loved ones. Or maybe you have a desperate need, and you are fasting in conjunction with prayer for supplication to God.

If you are not used to fasting, or you have gotten out of the discipline of fasting, start small. Skip one meal or skip your favorite drink for a day. Like prayer, the key is consistency. As you pray and seek God for more, you will be able to increase your fast, and you will have your flesh under subjection to your spirit.

Whatever the case may be, God will honor your fast and your sacrifice.

"Moreover, when ye fast, be not, as the hypocrites, of a sad countenance: for they disfigure their faces, that they may appear unto men to fast. Verily I say unto you, they have their reward. But thou, when thou fastest, anoint thine head, and wash thy face; that thou appear not unto men to fast, but unto thy Father which is in secret; and thy Father, which seeth in secret, shall reward thee openly."

Jesus

Matthew 6:16-18

Chapter Fourteen

Bible Study and Reading

If we desire to know God, we need to read and study His Word. In the pages of the Bible, His nature is revealed. I have heard some say, I wish God would speak to me. He has, in His Word.

To understand the Bible and the books of the Bible it is helpful to understand the purpose of each book and have a working knowledge of the point of each book.

Let's take a moment to step through the books of the Bible.

In the Old Testament, you will find thirty-nine books.

In Genesis through Deuteronomy, you will find the history of creation, the beginning of the Jewish race, and the Law of Moses presented by God.

From Joshua through Esther, you will read the history of Israel, the kings, prophets, and conflicts with other nations.

From Job through Song of Solomon, you will read poetry, love stories, and proverbs which are still very fitting for today.

The last seventeen books of the Old Testament, which are Isaiah through Malachi, are books of prophecy. Prophecies which cover the fate of Israel, the birth of the coming Messiah, judgment, tribulation, and the end of time. I believe many people who are not familiar with the Word of God, but who want to begin a reading program, at times can get bogged down in the Old Testament, because they are totally unfamiliar with it and find themselves lost in history and stories.

I have been asked by people, who are not familiar with the Bible, where they should begin to read to learn about Jesus and salvation as quickly as possible without getting bogged down. I always recommend starting in the gospel of John, which depicts Jesus as the Messiah and then proceed reading right into the book of Acts, which is the book following John. This will give the reader a working knowledge of who Jesus is and lead them into salvation. One can always go back to read the other three gospels.

Let's take a look at the New Testament, which has a total of twenty-seven books.

The first four books which are Matthew, Mark, Luke, and John, are the telling of the ministry of Jesus Christ. These books include his teachings concerning the new birth, also miracles, healings, the crucifixion, resurrection and ascension into heaven.

The fifth book, the book of Acts, is a history of the birth of the church on the day of Pentecost, and the ministries of the early church, including Apostle Peter, Apostle Paul, and others.

From Romans through Philippians, you'll find letters and teachings written by Apostle Paul giving direction and instruction to churches throughout the area, and individuals.

Hebrews through Jude are letters written by various authors, offering teaching, instruction and encouragement.

The final book of the Bible, Revelation, was written by John, the Apostle, while exiled on the isle of Patmos. Jesus Christ himself appeared to John and ordered him to write this letter to the seven churches of Asia. We have the opportunity to receive it ourselves. Much of the book is prophecies during the Tribulation which is coming to the Earth in the last days.

As you build the consistent, powerful prayer life you've always desired, add in fasting, mix in Bible reading or Bible study every day. You will be amazed at the transformation Jesus will bring to your spirit.

There are Bible reading programs available which will take you through the entire Bible in a year. Also available are Bible studies, some that you can work through on your own. There are more detailed studies as well, such as Search for Truth, or my favorite, Exploring God's Word, which is a twelve-lesson study leading the student through the entire Bible. Also, there are many Bible apps which can be downloaded onto any device, that can read the Bible to you. Many apps have helps that dig deeper into Biblical words and phrases. You may also find various Bible studies in many apps.

Whether you are brand new to the Bible or a seasoned Bible teacher, stay in the Word daily, along with prayer and consistent fasting. Through your efforts, God can take you to a level in Him you have never experienced and use you to win others to Him.

To find Godly reading material and Bible study material, I would suggest checking my publisher's website: woodsongpublishing.com and pentecostalpublishing.com

> "Study to shew thyself approved unto God, a workman that needeth not to be ashamed, rightly dividing the word of truth."
>
> Apostle Paul
>
> II Timothy 2:15

Chapter Fifteen

The Power of the Holy Ghost

While praying every day is the most powerful thing you can do for yourself, the Holy Ghost is the most powerful thing Jesus can do for you each day. He told his disciples before He ascended into heaven, "ye shall receive power, after that the Holy Ghost is come upon you" (Acts 1:8).

The Holy Ghost within us is the power that enables a follower of Christ to lay hands on the sick and see them healed. It is the power that enables us to perform miracles in the name of Jesus. It is the power that will resurrect us when Jesus returns for His church.

> But if the Spirit of him that raised up Jesus from the dead dwell in you, he that raised up Christ from the dead shall also quicken your mortal bodies by his Spirit that dwelleth in you.
>
> Romans 8:11

In John Chapter Fourteen, Jesus told His disciples He would not leave them comfortless, but He would come to them. There would be another Comforter that would come and be with them forever, the Spirit of Truth, who "dwells with you, but shall be IN you." Jesus was speaking of the Holy Ghost that was to fall upon them on the Day of Pentecost.

Luke tells us in his gospel that before ascending into the heavens, Jesus instructed them to go to Jerusalem and tarry until they be "endued with power," which comes by the infilling of the Holy Ghost.

So why did Jesus stress receiving "power," and what difference did it make in the lives of the believers according to the book of Acts?

The difference is like trying to get through life on your own strength and intellect as compared to being full of the power and anointing of God. On our own strength we are limited, but when we have the power of the Holy Ghost in our lives, we can do all things through Christ.

We can live our entire life on human ability and expertise, or we can live our life with the power of the Holy Ghost within, guiding us every day. The life being lived with human ability certainly could give us a nice life, but the life filled with the power of the Holy Ghost will bring healings, miracles, joy, and ultimately, salvation leading us to heaven.

Some of the benefits to submitting to Jesus and receiving His Spirit are:

- Spiritual empowerment to overcome temptation
- Opening our heart and mind to understand Scripture
- The use of Spiritual Gifts
- Producing Spiritual fruit, such as love, peace, and joy. (Galatians 5:22-23)

The one hundred twenty in the upper room (Acts 2:1-4) received the Holy Ghost with the evidence of speaking in tongues by being unified and praying together.

The believers that Apostle Philip preached to in Samaria (Acts 8:14-17) received the Holy Ghost after being baptized in Jesus Name and the ministry laid their hands on them praying.

Cornelius and his household and close friends all received the Holy

Ghost while hearing Apostle Peter preach the word (Acts 10:44-47).

When Apostle Paul entered Ephesus (Acts 19:5-6) he met twelve disciples of John the Baptist. After being baptized in Jesus Name, they came up out of the water and received the Holy Ghost when Paul laid his hands on them.

It is needful to pray every day, and it is good to have a discipline of fasting, but the real power to living an overcoming life in Jesus, is to be filled with the Holy Ghost with the evidence of speaking in tongues. This is the power Jesus was talking about in Acts 1:8.

In the book of Acts, there are at least twenty-nine mentions of healings, miracles, and widespread signs and wonders. These do not include every person who received the Holy Ghost with the evidence of speaking in tongues, or specific miraculous events not mentioned during missionary journeys. Keep in mind, every one of these occurrences happened not because Jesus was physically on the scene, but because He had filled His followers with power. He told His disciples that they would do greater things than He had done. (John 14:12).

I have long preached and taught that our churches today should look just like the church in the book of Acts. If a church is truly following Christ and His power, that church should see healings, miracles, and the power of the Holy Ghost brought down into the services and lives of the assembly regularly. If not, something is wrong.

Now, let's make it personal. How about you and me? If we have a Jesus obsession, we should be praying, fasting and seeking His power. With that being done, we should lay hands on the sick and see them healed. We should ask the Lord to do a certain thing, and it be done.

Luke writes in the nineteenth chapter of the Book of Acts concerning seven sons of a man named Sceva, who tried to cast out devils. They did not have the power of the Holy Ghost in them, and the evil spirits did not recognize them as men of God. They were attacked by the man possessed by devils, and he did great injury to these seven men, who were not prepared. It is because they had not been praying, fasting, and had not received God's power.

To receive the power of the Holy Ghost is not a difficult thing. We must believe that Christ is who He says He is. We must repent of our sins and ask the Lord to forgive us of those sins. We must be baptized in the Name of Jesus Christ for the remission of those sins (Acts 2:38), and then He has promised to fill us with the Holy Ghost. To receive the Holy Ghost, we must continue seeking Him. Some receive the Holy Ghost before being baptized, just as Cornelius and his household did.

My father received the Holy Ghost one Sunday afternoon in his bedroom seeking the Lord.

I'll never forget my teenage friend who received the Holy Ghost the very first time he attended an Apostolic Pentecostal church service, after feeling the power of God for the first time.

I witnessed a demon possessed man be delivered from the devils that had him bound and then immediately receive the Holy Ghost.

One of my very own grandsons received the Holy Ghost at eight years old during kid's church on a Wednesday night.

While prayer is the relationship, and fasting is the sacrifice, the Holy Ghost is the power, the jet fuel, the fire, that enables the child of God to reach a level that many do not know.

> "You cannot possess anything you are unwilling to pursue."
>
> Bishop Jeff Arnold
>
> "And these signs shall follow them that believe. In my name shall they cast out devils, they shall speak with new tongues, they shall take up serpents, and if they drink any deadly thing, it shall not hurt them, they

shall lay hands on the sick, and they shall recover."

Jesus

Mark 16:37,38

Chapter Sixteen
Attitudes

I have preached and taught for many years that while prayer, fasting, Bible study, and church attendance are very important, a large part of living a victorious life in Christ is our attitude. If a person has a defeatist attitude, or is constantly looking for something to be wrong, you are defeated already.

In living life, you find whatever it is you are looking for. If you are looking for good news, blessings, and some sunshine in your day, you will find it. If you wake up every morning and wonder what's going to go wrong today, you'll find plenty to complain about.

I'm not talking about the man-made mindset of positive thinking, happy thinking, magical thinking, or the like. I'm telling you, if Jesus has forgiven you of your sins, set your path in accordance to His will, and is shining His love upon you, why would you lie in a muddy ditch? Get up and get excited about what God is doing in your life.

If your car breaks down, thank God you have a car. If your roof begins to leak, thank God you have a house. If you become sick, thank God for those thousands of days He blessed you with good health. There will always be bad news to challenge our faith, but there's always good news to show us how blessed we are.

When we come to Jesus, He changes us. One of the things He changes is our minds.

> "I beseech you therefore, brethren, by the mercies of God, that ye present your bodies a living sacrifice, holy, acceptable unto God, which is your reasonable

> service. And be not conformed to this world but be ye transformed by the renewing of your mind, that ye may prove what is that good, and acceptable and perfect, will of God."
>
> Apostle Paul
>
> Romans 12:1-2

Even when I was young and just beginning to read the Bible, I noticed what Paul said there. Renewing our minds can be transformable. Just changing our mindset can transform us. Some people live their lives under a dark cloud simply because they refuse to change their attitude. That is not what Jesus intends for us.

Every person Jesus touched during His earthly ministry had a changed mindset after His touch. Notice after their encounter with Jesus, they rejoiced, they praised Him, they followed Him, they testified of His goodness. This is the will of God.

When you had your first encounter with Jesus, did you not smile, or cry from happiness? Your heart was transformed, so your mind should be transformed as well: a renewing. A better, or more positive attitude.

When we have His Spirit in us, it transforms us from the old man and into the new man in Christ. See Ephesians 4:22-24. The more we grow in Him, the more we gain His attributes. Our hearts and minds are changed because of His Spirit, and we do not think or talk as we used to, before Christ. We begin to put forth fruit which is like Christ.

> But the fruit of the Spirit is love, joy, peace, longsuffering, gentleness, goodness, faith, meekness, temperance: against such there is no law. And they that are Christ's have crucified the flesh with the affections and lusts.
>
> Galatians 5:22-24

These are the attributes we should display after an encounter with Jesus. I'll admit, some of these may take time and practice. We don't become perfect just because we have received the Holy Ghost, but we should take on the attributes of Christ as we crucify our flesh, affections and lust.

We need to guard our hearts from negative thinking and attitudes. Let us strive to have an optimistic, positive attitude in our daily lives, with the fruit of the Spirit springing forth from our lives. As children of God, we have much to be thankful for, and I refuse to live in darkness, when He has promised me a mansion one day. Let us live with an attitude of thanksgiving and a heart filled with praise.

> "I will extoll [*praise enthusiastically*] thee, my God, O King: And I will bless thy name forever and ever. Every day will I bless thee; And I will praise thy name forever and ever. Great is the Lord, and greatly to be praised; And his greatness is unsearchable. One generation shall praise thy works to another, and shall declare thy mighty acts. I will speak of the glorious honor of thy majesty, and thy wondrous works."
>
> David, King of Israel
>
> Psalm 145:1-5

Chapter Seventeen

The Gifts of the Spirit

In his second letter to the church in Corinth, Apostle Paul instructed that we should "follow after charity (love) and desire spiritual gifts." He then proceeded to give instruction on the proper use of Spiritual Gifts. It is not the purpose of this chapter to teach concerning Spiritual Gifts, but rather I hope to inspire you to seek the Lord in deeper ways than perhaps you have.

I personally believe that Spiritual Gifts are not in operation in denominational type churches because the pastor, or church leadership, does not believe it is possible today, or the ministry of the church does not teach it for the edifying (instruction) of the church body. Another reason perhaps is because the pastor or ministerial leadership has not completely submitted to God and received the power of the Holy Ghost, therefore Spiritual Gifts cannot operate through them.

Spiritual Gifts are seen in Apostolic Pentecostal churches, but not all. Why would that be? Again, personally I believe when we have an Apostolic Pentecostal church where Spiritual Gifts are never, or rarely displayed, it may be because the pastor or ministerial leadership are not consecrated enough to be used by the Spirit to these depths. Spiritual Gifts are not the same as repenting and being baptized, or receiving the baptism of the Holy Ghost.

When we come to the Lord and dedicate our lives to follow Him, we do certain things to accomplish our spiritual goal. We pray, we fast, we read our Bible, and attend church services. These are things everyone who desires to be a child of God should do. Spiritual Gifts are specific. They are Spirit empowered abilities that God gifts to a person for that time to perform the miraculous in the church service, or for a special need. For example, probably the most common seen Spiritual Gift is healing of the body. I cannot tell you how many people I have seen in my life that have been prayed for and received immediate healing from Jesus, including me on several occasions.

The purpose of Spiritual Gifts is not to build up a specific person but rather encourage and teach the body of Christ, through such things as teaching, healing, prophecy, or discernment. Spiritual Gifts should be visible, active, and functioning to meet specific needs within the church assembly.

Now here's the catch. The Lord distributes Spiritual Gifts according to His will. He is a Sovereign God and works through whom He will. Not every believer has a Spiritual Gift, or is used in Spiritual Gifts.

I included this chapter concerning Spiritual Gifts simply to inspire you and encourage you to not just seek Jesus for salvation but seek Him for depth of relationship. Yes, we desire to be ready when He returns for His church, but I want to encourage you to be ready to be used of God. Not simply in your talents that he has blessed you with, such as singing, playing an instrument, or teaching, but deeper than your own abilities.

The Lord may never use you in the Gifts of the Spirit, but He seeks people He can use. I'm sure you want to be prepared.

In the book of Acts, Spiritual Gifts were used many times, including miracles or prophecies performed through Peter, Philip, Paul, Agabus, and others. Since we have the same Lord and Savior, and the same Spirit working in us, we too should see these gifts used in us and in our churches today.

Continue to dig deeply into the presence of Jesus. Pray, fast, and get into the Word. You may one day be surprised how the Lord may use you for His kingdom.

> "Set your affection on things above, not on things on the earth."
>
> Apostle Paul
>
> Colossians 3:2

Chapter Eighteen

Honoring God

As we grow in the strength of Jesus, through the power He has given us, we are called to live a life that honors Him. In Matthew chapter five, Jesus commanded, "Let your light so shine before men, that they may see your good works, and glorify your Father which is in heaven."

When Matthew wrote his gospel, he used the Greek word "doxazosin," which was later translated into English for our benefit as "glorify." This word means to render glory, honor, or bestow honor. The root word "doxa," conveys praising or magnifying God. Jesus was literally commanding us to live a life that brings glory and honor to Him, and by doing so, others will give glory and honor to Him as well.

We honor God by living a life that matches everything we claim to be. So many in our society claim to be a Christian but do not display the life or attributes Jesus taught. To be a Christian is to be "like Christ." When a person comes to Jesus and repents of their sin, it is not the finished product, but the beginning.

As we study His Word, and grow in Him, we begin to talk and act differently than we did before. There are words or phrases we may have used when we lived in sin, but now the Word and His Spirit may quicken us to change our language. There may be places we frequented, while in the world, that the Spirit now keeps us from visiting.

We honor God by being a good steward with the resources He has blessed us with. By giving our employer an honest day's work for what we have agreed to for payment. We honor God by being a good neighbor to those who live near us. We honor God by presenting ourselves in holiness and not as the world.

Cultivating a lifestyle of gratitude, serving others through acts of kindness, love, and community, honors God. We honor God by giving compassion, grace, and forgiveness, just as Jesus gave us. We even honor Him when we speak life and encouragement into those who are discouraged.

Apostle Paul instructs us in I Corinthians 7:14 that an unbelieving husband, or an unbelieving wife, is sanctified by their believing spouse. Paul uses the Greek word "hegiastai" which is the passive indicative form of "hagiazo" which means set apart or made holy. By living holy and honoring the Lord in front of your unsaved spouse, your life plays a very important role in them coming to the Lord. You could win your unbelieving spouse to Jesus by simply honoring God in your daily life.

> Honor the Lord with thy substance, and with the firstfruits of all thine increase.
>
> Proverbs 3:9

When we support the work of God by giving to missions, our local assembly, and other ministries with our tithing and offerings, we are honoring God.

> "I beseech you therefore, brethren, by the mercies of God, that ye present your bodies a living sacrifice, holy, acceptable unto God, which is your reasonable service."
>
> Apostle Paul
>
> Romans 12:1

I believe it would be a righteous thing for us to wake up every morning and ask ourselves, "How can I honor God today?" You see, being obsessed with Jesus is not about you and me, it's about Him.

It's not about what He can do for us, but rather what we can do daily to draw closer to Him. Apostle Paul says it's reasonable, and I agree.

What are other ways we honor God?

- We honor God when we keep our commitment to prayer, fasting and Bible reading
- We honor God by regular church attendance
- We honor God when we respect and honor His anointed
- We honor God when we teach our children to honor Him and respect the things of God
- We honor God when we live holy as an example to those in our lives
- We honor God when we witness and win others to Christ

Honoring God is not just the huge things we think of in life. It's also every small decision we make throughout our day. It's the small acts we perform when we don't even realize people are watching. It's the things we say and do that we soon forget, but others remember.

> Thou art worthy, O Lord, to receive glory and honor and power: for thou hast created all things, and for thy pleasure they are and were created.
>
> Revelation 4:11

Chapter Nineteen
The Battle

We need to understand that anytime we seek to draw closer to the Lord, or live a victorious life in Him, we will face obstacles thrown in our way by the enemy. The enemy, Satan, who will attempt to toy with our mind, tempt us with sin, and cause distractions in our life.

If the devil cannot destroy us with sin, he will try his best to keep us distracted. There are many distractions in this world. In our dedication to prayer, regular fasting, faithful church attendance, and giving, we must stay aware of the enemy's tactics.

We may feel secure in what we are doing because we have not openly sinned against God, but have we given the Lord all the time He deserves? If we are not careful, we may find ourselves scrolling on social media when we should be praying. Harmless entertainment could be taking away from Bible reading or studying. Social media and entertainment are not necessarily sinful, but like fishing, hunting, hiking, and many more enjoyable activities, they can become harmful to our walk with God if they interfere with our dedication.

I don't have statistics to back this up, but I believe the failure of many people of God is not open sin, but distraction. We walk into the church doors on Sunday and realize we are not prepared for the service. Not because we have lived in sin all week, but we have been distracted with what felt like life, and we have not prayed and made ourselves ready.

To be obsessed with Jesus means to make Him the center of all we say, think and do. That's not to say we can't have hobbies and do enjoyable things with our family and children, but we must acquire an acute sense of not being distracted. We must understand that prayer, fasting, and being spiritually sensitive are important aspects of our lives that we must not allow to fail.

Now that we have covered distraction, let's go to the second thing I'd like to cover, so we are aware. There are times in life we face an all out attack from Satan. Unlike distractions, which we can easily handle if we stay aware, attacks of Satan come from the outside, and demand our response.

Oddly enough, I have seen people who are not living for God face terrible illness or diversity, and it drives them to Jesus. I have seen people seemingly living a victorious life, face illness or diversity, and it drives them away from Jesus, as though they blame Him. We must have our minds made up. In this life we will face illnesses and attacks, but we must remember, all good things come from above. Jesus will get you through every battle if you will completely trust Him.

Attacks from Satan can come in various forms and various strengths. Apostle Paul, as mentioned in the chapter covering his life, faced attacks from Satan, attacks from brethren, and tragedies such as shipwreck. He never blamed God for any of these adversities.

I'm going to share with you a conversation I had with the Lord many years ago. I hesitate because it's rather embarrassing, and it's not a "feel good" story. But I feel led to share it in this chapter to help someone.

I was going through a very rough time, and I didn't understand why I had to go through it. I was rather unhappy with the situation and decided to express my displeasure to the Lord in prayer. While praying, I reminded the Lord of what I had done for the kingdom, the teaching and preaching, the home Bible studies I've taught. I had the attitude that I didn't deserve to be going through the situation that had presented itself.

The Spirit interrupted my prayer and said very clearly, "Are you better than Peter? Are you better than John? Are you better than Paul?"

I immediately felt ashamed and realized how I must have sounded to the Lord. I said, "Lord, I get it" and then proceeded to back out of that conversation as quickly as possible. Learning my lesson, I have not complained to the Lord about anything since that day.

The truth is, God has given us all the weaponry we need to overcome. He has given us defensive weapons and offensive weapons. Apostle Paul, in writing to the church in Ephesus instructed them to "be strong in the Lord, and in the power of his might" (Ephesians 6:1).

You see, the power, or victories, don't come from our own might anyway. We are helpless to fight against the power of the enemy on our own strength. God has given us everything we need to overcome. We simply need to know what weapons are available to us and use them.

> For though we walk in the flesh, we do not war after the flesh (for the weapons of our warfare are not carnal, but mighty through God to the pulling down of strong holds).
>
> II Corinthians 10: 3-4

Apostle Paul told us that we do not fight against flesh and blood, but against principalities against powers, against rulers of darkness of this world, against spiritual wickedness in high places. (Ephesians 6:12) The only option we have in defeating Satan and his powers when they come against us is to have on the armor of God. He has given us everything we need. We simply need to take advantage of it.

Let me encourage you, that when Satan comes against you in your spirit or life, fight against him with anointing and fervor. Don't be passive. [Fer-vor; intense and passionate feeling]

The Lord will many times not release you from your battle but will allow you to fight your way out of it. Just as the little weakling on the beach we've read about over the years must go to the gym day after day to get strong, to overcome the bully, likewise, we must fight our spiritual battles to gain strength in our spirit. Many times our battles become our ministry or testimony. If the Lord rescued us every time we had a problem, without us fighting our way through it, we would not have the ministry or testimony that we now have.

> The nearer you get to the promise, the harder the battle.
>
> T.F. Tenny

> Submit yourselves therefore to God. Resist the devil, and he will flee from you. Draw nigh to God, and he will draw nigh to you.
>
> James 4:7-8

I have heard people over my life proclaim, "resist the devil, and he will flee from you," but that doesn't work. James says to first submit yourself to God. I hate to say this out loud, but the devil is not afraid of you. He's not afraid of me either. When we submit ourselves to God, cover ourselves in baptism by His Name, and receive the power of the Holy Ghost, he fears us, because we are covered by the blood of Jesus. James added the promise that if we draw near to God, He will draw near to us.

The third and last point I want to bring out, talking about our battle, is our flesh. We blame a lot on the devil, but I believe we human beings wrestle with ourselves much more than we wrestle with Satan. Our biggest challenge is that person we see in the mirror every morning. If we could keep that person in line, a lot of our problems and battles would go away.

You see, we are a spirit being. God deals with us through our spirit. It is our spirit that responds to His calling and His ways. When He fills us with the baptism of the Holy Ghost He fills our spirit, or soul. We just happen to be wrapped in carnal flesh which constantly wars against the Spirit.

> This I say then, walk in the Spirit, and ye shall not fulfil the lust of the flesh. For the flesh lusteth against the Spirit, and the Spirit against the flesh, and these are contrary the one to the other, so that ye cannot do the things that ye would.
>
> Galatians 5:16-17

The only way to defeat the flesh is to walk in the Spirit. As fleshly beings, we are naturally driven by the desires of the flesh. In other words, it is the nature of the flesh to do whatever it wants to do. That fleshly urge is defeated by prayer, fasting, and submitting ourselves to God.

Realize there is power through a life of disciplined prayer and fasting. It is important to read the Word of God and hear Bible studies to learn what Jesus expects of you. Never underestimate the power of the Name of Jesus, and the blood of the Lamb by which you are covered.

As you seek to grow deeper and stronger in the Lord and become obsessed with living for Him and pleasing Him, carnal people will not understand your life. That's okay, they didn't understand Jesus either.

My prayer for you, taken from the words of Paul, the Apostle.

> "For this cause I bow my knees unto the Father of our Lord Jesus Christ, of whom the whole family in heaven and earth is named, that he would grant you, according to the riches of his glory, to be strengthened with might by his Spirit in the inner man; that Christ may dwell in your hearts by faith; that ye, being rooted and grounded in love, may be able to

comprehend with all saints what is the breadth, and length, and depth, and height; and to know the love of Christ, which passeth knowledge, that ye might be filled with all the fullness of God. Now unto him that is able to do exceeding abundantly above all that we ask or think, according to the power that worketh in us, unto him be glory in the church by Christ Jesus throughout all ages, world without end. Amen."

Apostle Paul

Ephesians 3:14-21

www.ingramcontent.com/pod-product-compliance
Lightning Source LLC
LaVergne TN
LVHW010936110826
845149LV00013B/2627

* 9 7 8 1 9 6 1 4 8 2 2 8 9 *